SCULPTING THE LAND

Landscape design influenced by abstract art

Parco Franco Verga, Milan : image by Milano Panoramica

SCULPTING THE LAND

Landscape design influenced by abstract art

Diana Armstrong Bell

Unicorn

Published in 2019 by
Unicorn, an imprint of Unicorn Publishing Group LLP
5 Newburgh Street
London
W1F 7RG

www.unicornpublishing.org

ISBN 978-1-912690-46-6

10 9 8 7 6 5 4 3 2 1

Designed by Diana Armstrong Bell
Printed in Europe for Latitude Press Ltd

Acknowledgements

This book is a curated collection of eleven of my projects that, I feel have art at their core. My thanks to **Rose de Jardin** and **Professor Martin Bryant** who both encouraged me to write this book.

I will always be profoundly thankful to **David Johnston** at Arup, who supported me in my first competition entry for Lac de Sénart, France and for believing that we could win. This led to all the projects which followed and everything shown in this book.

My special thanks to **Richard Carman** who has produced all the beautiful perspective visualisations, hand-drawn and watercoloured, which are illustrated in this volume. Richard started visualising my projects when I won Parco Franco Verga, Milan and our collaboration has continued. The drawings help to make my work explicable; he has brought a great deal to my practice and I am truly grateful. Many thanks also to all who have worked for Armstrong Bell Landscape Design over the years and helped to make these projects possible, and to my clients and the design teams on the projects as credited, who have all contributed to their realisation. Special thanks to architects **John Muir and Martyn Kemp** who invited me to work on several projects shown in this book.

I am grateful to **Gordon Citrine** who has patiently helped me with his technical expertise throughout the making of this book and also to **Neil Smith** for his visualisations, all hand-drawn in ink for Lac de Sénart. Many thanks to **Oliver Moss** at Depot-Designers for designing the book cover.

Working abroad can be stimulating but also challenging. I owe much to the help of my former students **Simon Le Coeur** who helped me with translations and client meetings in Paris and to **Laura Baratta** and her family in Milan, who were all enormously supportive and hospitable when I was working on Parco Franco Verga.

The Zaha Hadid Foundation kindly and with overwhelming generosity allowed me access to drawings for The Peak project in Hong Kong. My warmest thanks for enabling me to pay tribute to Zaha Hadid by showing her work in my book. I wish to thank **Julia Barfield** of Marks Barfield Architects, for her generosity in permitting me to use images prepared by her practice, for Clapham Gateway.

I am grateful to **Milano Panoramica** for the exceptional images of the Milan park which show the scale of the project and how its realisation matches the drawings. Also, many thanks to **Bill Blake** as credited in the book, whose photographs illustrate my belief that landscape can be art.

Hal Moggridge kindly introduced me to **Lord Ian Strathcarron of Unicorn Publishing,** who agreed to publish my book. Many thanks to Ian for guiding me through the early stages of preparing this book and to his team for keeping me going. My thanks also to **Elizabeth Wilhide** for her invaluable advice at the outset of this project.

Finally, an enormous thank you to **Richard Stone,** my encourager, supporter, sounding board, listener and advisor, whose help, humour and belief in this book have sustained me throughout the long hours of toil.

Diana Armstrong Bell

Diana founded her award-winning practice, Armstrong Bell Landscape Design, in 1984 and works internationally across the Middle East, Europe and the UK, with a focus on large-scale public landscapes in the urban realm, with many of the landscapes being created on brownfield sites.

She is known for distinctive, innovative designs that are site-specific and sensitive to context, pushing the usual boundaries of landscape architecture. Contemporary designs for urban parks and spaces, many of which have won international design competitions, show the influence of Diana's background in art and design, particularly her study of abstract art. She believes in the value of drawing by hand as a means of developing and presenting ideas.

Diana taught Landscape Architecture at the University of Greenwich and at The Inchbald School of Design, and she lectures widely in the UK and Europe. In 2002, she was invited by the Comune di Milano, to participate in judging the international competition for Parco Forlanini, Milan. She contributes to international publications and books including *The Oxford Companion to the Garden* edited by Patrick Taylor and *Cinque Paesaggisti per Milano,* where her work is profiled.

Diana studied Art, followed by Landscape Architecture, at Gloucestershire College of Art and Design, where she won the Gane Trust Travel Scholarship, enabling her to spend a summer in Italy studying townscape in Siena. She is a chartered member of the Landscape Institute.

Image : Pat Stockley

Contents

Introduction

Sculpting the Land, shows a selection of large-scale public landscapes, many of which have won international design competitions and are influenced by abstract art, particularly the work of Kazimir Malevich

The idea of sculpting the land led me into landscape architecture which, I have always held, is one of the arts. Drawn to the sculptural and painterly qualities of the natural and farmed landscape, where earthworks, lines and patterns can appear over time almost as land art, it is important to spend time observing, listening and gathering clues about the landscape's past and how it informs a new story.

An early inspiration came with a visit to Carlo Scarpa's cemetery for the Brion family at San Vito, Italy. It appeared almost as a collection of responses tooled in concrete and set in a landscape, each connected as a journey of remembrances. It was a poetic and artistic response which captured feelings in the built form.

Abstract art has always been an influence, a means of enriching my design thinking. The work of the Suprematist artist Kazimir Malevich and his associates, Moholy-Nagy and El Lissitzky, can be read as a notation for the design of cities and landscapes. Applying this thinking to the organisation of landscapes, to the manipulation of earth form, groups of trees and built structures has resulted in unusual designs. As the shape of the design emerges, it is constantly checked against the brief requirements, the particularity and character of the site and its context and functionality.

The work of Architect Zaha Hadid, has been an enduring influence on my design thinking since I saw her project for The Peak, Hong Kong, in the 1980's, which is discussed and illustrated in the following pages.

Visiting Paris in 1990, where I looked at contemporary architecture projects, followed by Barcelona a few years later, where I saw new public landscapes which seemed to have art at their core, convinced me that it was time for a radical shift in landscape design thinking in the UK. Our great historic landscapes by Capability Brown, Repton and others were cutting edge in their day yet there seemed to be an apparent reluctance to move on from the typology of historicism and classicism in landscape design. I felt it was time for a re-think when an opportunity arose to design new landscapes which are not part of a historic setting.

Searching for opportunities to design large-scale contemporary landscapes, I decided to enter design competitions. Winning my first European competition for a new urban park at Lac de Sénart, France in 1992 led to numbers of further competitions for public landscapes in the urban realm, some of which are shown in this book.

Designs drawn by hand in pencil and ink, collage, watercolour and modelling are used to develop and present schemes. The presentation plans and visualisations are regarded as more than simply conveyors of information; they embody a series of ideas and are regarded as a form of art.

This re-invention of the landscape design process and allowing art to influence the outcome led to an original and contemporary approach to landscape design, which resulted in winning six international design competitions and being a finalist in a further three.

Concept visualisation showing sculpted
earth at Parco Franco Verga, Milan

Introduction : *Sculpting the Land*

Inspirations and Influences

Abstract Art : Kazimir Malevich and Suprematism

The influence of abstact art has led to re-imagining the spatial arrangement of new landscapes

Malevich's Suprematist paintings explore the spatial relationships between elements, which are visually deconstructed, fluid and layered. The format emphasises neither the vertical nor the horizontal, which brings a dynamism to the works. The movement of one line or element alters the whole and creates a new dynamic. These paintings can be read as a notation for the design of cities, landscapes and buildings.

The painting opposite is reminiscent of an urban space, where the red and black squares on the right and the black rectangle at bottom left hold the space between them, in much the same way as buildings might. The space is cut by a diagonal red line which could denote movement through the space.

My designs use these ideas to organise the spatial arrangement of landscapes; in so doing, unusual abstract geometries are created. Designs start using collage where the relationships between objects in the design can remain fluid until a satisfactory relationship of elements is achieved. Using art as an inspiration in this way is all about looking. Time spent observing these works leads to an understanding of the visual language that Malevich developed, which can then be applied to landscape design. Particular paintings do not associate with any given landscape, rather they influence a different approach to design as a whole.

Kazimir Malevich : *Suprematist Non-Objective Composition*, 1915 : Oil on canvas

Kazimir Malevich : Abstract Art : Inspirations and Influences

Kazimir Malevich : *Suprematist Painting*, 1916 : Oil on canvas

Kazimir Malevich : *Supremus No. 50*, 1915 : Oil on canvas

Kazimir Malevich : Abstract Art : Inspirations and Influences

Zaha Hadid Architects

The Peak : Hong Kong
1982–83

The architecture for this cliff-top resort was conceived as a Suprematist geology. Materials impact vertically and horizontally, the building is stratified, each layer defining a function. Drawings and paintings are used to visualise ideas of dynamism, abstraction and fragmentation, inspired by Malevich and the Suprematist artists of the Russian avant-garde.

'The architecture is like a knife cutting through the site. It cuts through traditional principles of organistaion and reconstitutes new ones, defies nature and resists destroying it.'
Zaha Hadid Architects

I have followed the work of Zaha Hadid closely since seeing The Peak project in the 1980s, inspired and influenced by her approach to re-imagining the organisation of space, by her confidence to cast aside traditional principles of spatial design and by her regard for art as a means of inspiring architecture. She has quite simply been a guiding light in my own design journey.

This page : *Blue Slabs* by Zaha Hadid
Detail drawings in black and white by Zaha Hadid
Opposite : *Painting 738* by Zaha Hadid
Site plan in black and white

All the images shown are Courtesy of the Zaha Hadid Foundation

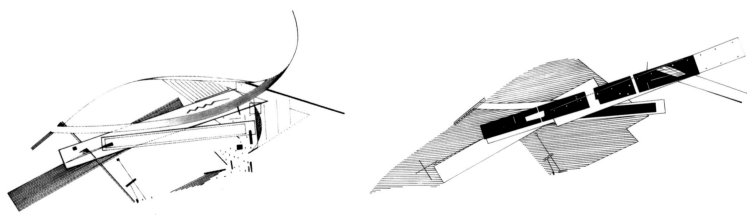

Zaha Hadid : Architecture : Inspirations and Influences

Earthworks, lines and patterns in the landscape

Drawing on the sculptural and painterly qualities of the natural and farmed landscape to inspire new designs

The landscape has been sculpted with a purpose for millennia. The patterns of the past have left imprints on the surface of the land. Now these marks, lines and forms appear almost as though they are abstract interventions scattered across the landscape and yet each hold their own human story. Landscape is a memory bank of human and animal happenings etched on to the surface of the land. Many are so subtle that they appear only when the sun is low and shadows are cast. Over time, these landforms can appear almost as a form of land art. Lines in the landscape, trees, ditches, dykes, field patterns, people tracks and animal tracks can appear as an abstract geometry of texture and colour. New landscapes can draw on the patterns of a place, connect with the past, yet create a new chapter in an evolving story.

Manea Fifties Looking North
Kite Aerial Photography by Bill Blake Heritage Documentation

Earthworks, Lines and Patterns in the Landscape : Inspirations and Influences

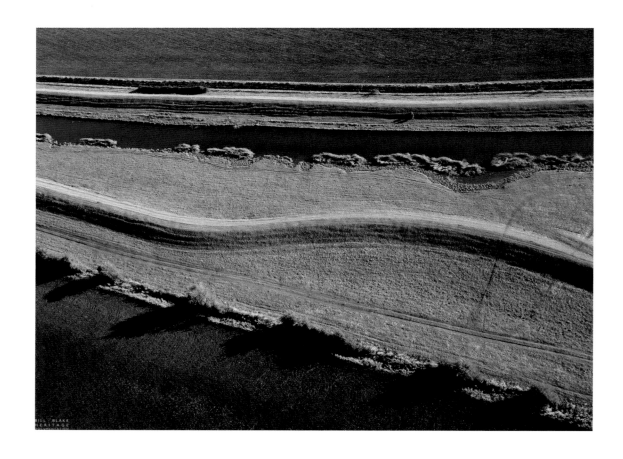

Old West River Flood Bank : an abstract geometry of lines

Opposite top : Earith KAP
Bottom right : Warham Camp detail
Bottom left : Bartlow Hills
All images above and opposite
Kite Aerial Photography by Bill Blake Heritage Documentation

Earthworks, Lines and Patterns in the Landscape : Inspirations and Influences

Trees

Trees in cities are green architecture, they make cities liveable

Trees are the green building blocks in the urban environment. They can establish spatial boundaries, create the walls and ceilings of outdoor rooms and give urban space a sense of human scale. Trees are a green web threading through our cities. They can reduce the impact of roads by turning footpaths into green corridors; they extend the geometry and rhythm of buildings into the landscape. They mark the changing seasons and bring us closer to nature. Trees make cities liveable.

Ancient trees can inspire awe, even humility. Old oaks, knarled and twisted, become living sculptures; they date our landscapes and connect us with our past. Single specimen trees, a cherry tree laden with blossom or the lush leaves of a *Paulownia* on a street corner, can become local icons.

Trees used to 'green' cities can help to mitigate the negatives of pollution, climate change and loss of habitat but aesthetic awareness is still crucial to design with trees and lift our responses above the purely pragmatic. The following images illustrate trees used with a sense of purpose to create outdoor rooms, green corridors or just delightful places to pause. They tend to show assemblages of single species which can create a more powerful effect than a 'pick and mix' of species.

In parks and open spaces, trees can be used to define space, create vision corridors and give structure. Groups of trees can bring flow and informality; they can weave their way through structural groupings of trees or built structures.

Trees can live for centuries and along with landform, they are the most important and enduring ingredients of a landscape designer's palette.

An oak tree marks the changing seasons

Images : Gordon Citrine

Trees : Inspirations and Influences

A walk through Boboli Gardens in Florence, where trees and hedges line walks, focus
views and create shade, shelter and delight. This classical garden shows principles
which can be re-imagined in contemporary schemes.

Images this page and opposite : Diana Armstrong Bell

Trees, shadow and light in this informal design at the Villa Aldobrandini, Italy

Trees : Inspirations and Influences

The National Gallery
Sainsbury Wing, London

The National Gallery

Sainsbury Wing Piazza, London

Plane trees mirror the scale of adjacent buildings; this is tree planting
used as green architecture

Planted in grids, rows and avenues, trees create patterns that are woven into the fabric of a city. I first realised this when I was in Paris many years ago. Place des Vosges is a classic example of how trees can make spaces. Planted in a tight grid, the trees become a room, the sense of place is powerful. As I wandered the streets of Paris, I realised that grids were connected to avenues and lines of trees. Occasionally, resting at a street corner wherever there was a slight widening, a pause point, a special individual tree was planted. Almost like a jewel on a black dress, a *Catalpa* or *Paulownia*, their immense exotic leaves would delight the walker. This was green architecture, used purposefully to bond a city together.

The Sainsbury Wing Piazza is the space which slides between the old gallery building and the new wing designed by Robert Venturi and Denise Scott Brown. The piazza is part of the Jubilee Walk which links Trafalgar Square with Leicester Square. A constant stream of people wander through the space, all day long. It is a movement space but also a space to pause and reflect.

The landscape layout takes its cue from the style and scale of the gallery buildings. It is simple and classical, using York stone and granite laid in an orthogonal pattern. Six plane trees, planted in a grid, furnish the space. The trees were sourced at Von Ehren Nursery in Germany as semi-mature specimens 5 m tall with cube heads. The day the trees arrived on site, the road to the rear was closed and each tree was lifted into the space by crane. When all six were planted, the space was transformed. It suddenly became an outdoor room, enclosed by the gallery walls with the plane trees forming the ceiling. What had seemed like an odd piece of 'land left over', assumed an identity. It became a space where you might linger on your walk through.

This design is now thirty years old yet it has stood the test of time. Quality paving has withstood intensive use but, most of all, this is a story about urban trees. The choice of plane trees mirrors the scale of the adjacent buildings; the grid formation is architectural. This is planting used as green architecture where trees are place makers.

CREDITS
Client : National Gallery Services
Architects : Venturi and Scott Brown
Associated Architects : Sheppard Robson
Landscape Architects : Armstrong Bell Landscape Design
Structural Consultants : Ove Arup and Partners
Date : 1989-90

Sainsbury Wing : The National Gallery, London

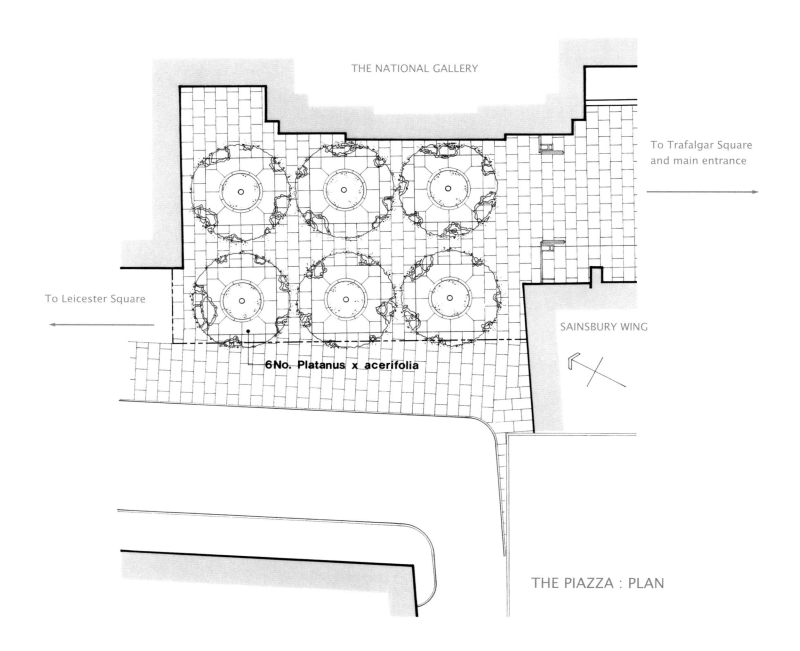

THE NATIONAL GALLERY

To Trafalgar Square
and main entrance

To Leicester Square

6No. Platanus x acerifolia

SAINSBURY WING

THE PIAZZA : PLAN

Sainsbury Wing : The National Gallery, London

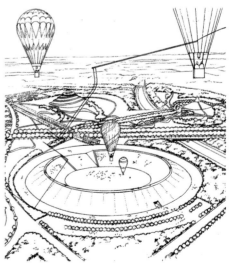

Lac de Sénart
France

Lac de Sénart, Melun-Sénart, France

Sculpting 4 million cubic metres of spoil, to create a park as the centrepiece of the new town was the brief for this design competition

This 135-ha park and a 40-ha lake were planned as the central focus of the new town of Melun-Sénart. Four million cubic metres of spoil were to be dug out to create the lake. An international design competition was launched to find a design which used this vast amount of spoil to create a series of sculpural earth formations, including an amphitheatre.

My landscape strategy, for our winning design, used the ancient hunting route, the Allée Royale, along with two further axes to structure the site. The levels were built up in a series of broad steps which were then sculpted into more subtle landforms. Modelling clay was used to design the landform whilst manually calculating the quantity of spoil that was being used. Eventually, the cut and fill quantities were calculated accurately by Arup.

Two large earth formations, the amphitheatre and a ziggurat are placed at either side of the Allée Royale. ·A stream flanked by an arboretum cuts through the strong axial path system, in a sinuous curve, creating a ribbon of colour against the green.

The Allée Royale was designed as a broad boulevard with a double row of beech trees. The path rises out of the ground on an embankment which bridges across the lakeside road to arrive at the restaurant terrace on the roof of the sailing school. The second axis rises out of the ground to meet the Allée Royale at its elevated level.

Following the competition, we were commissioned to develop the scheme, including planting and earth modelling strategies. Eventually, a change in local politics and a new town mayor led to plans for the new town being changed and the park was no longer required. However, this project led to a series of further competitions, many of which are shown in this book.

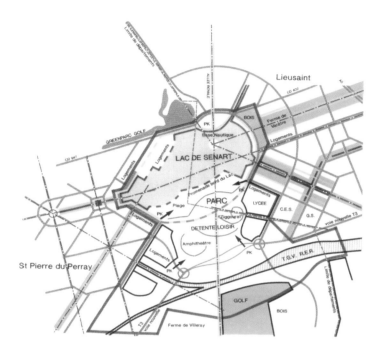

Central area of the new town with the lake and park
Plan by client : EPAMS

CREDITS
Client : Établissement public d'aménagement de Melun-Sénart
Landscape Architects : Armstrong Bell Landscape Design
Consulting Engineers : Arup
Date : 1992 competition, 1993 commission

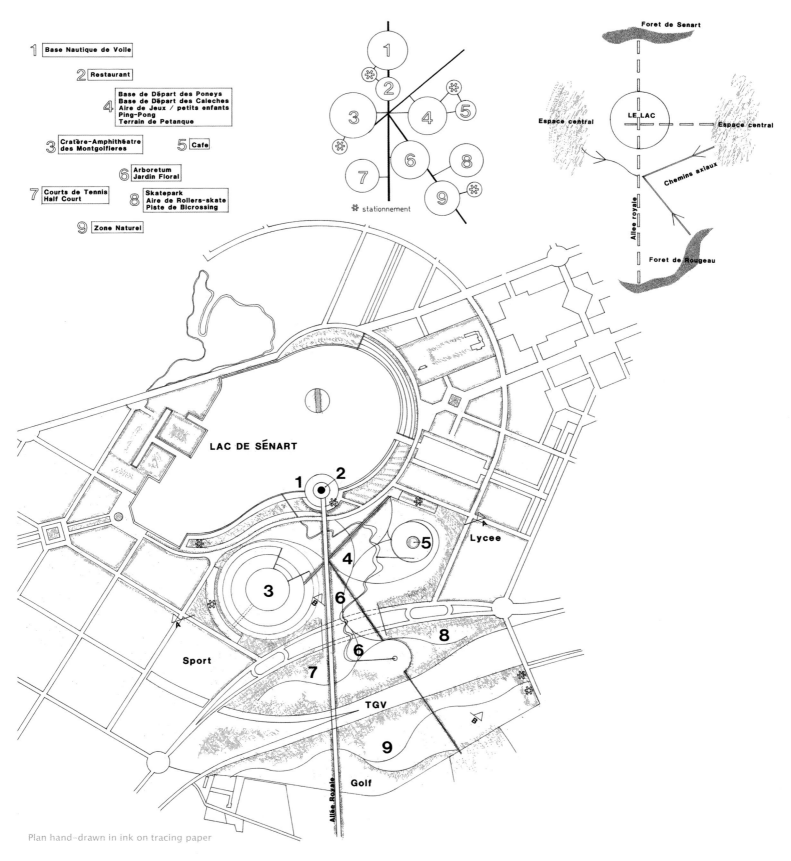

1 Base Nautique de Voile

2 Restaurant

4 Base de Départ des Poneys
Base de Départ des Caleches
Aire de Jeux / petits enfants
Ping-Pong
Terrain de Petanque

3 Cratère-Amphithéatre des Montgolfieres

5 Cafe

6 Arboretum Jardin Floral

7 Courts de Tennis Half Court

8 Skatepark
Aire de Rollers-skate
Piste de Bicrossing

9 Zone Naturel

※ stationnement

Foret de Senart

Espace central   LE LAC   Espace central

Chemins axiaux

Allee royale

Foret de Rougeau

LAC DE SÉNART

Lycee

Sport

TGV

Golf

Allée Royale

Plan hand-drawn in ink on tracing paper

Analysis and Activities : Lac de Sénart, France

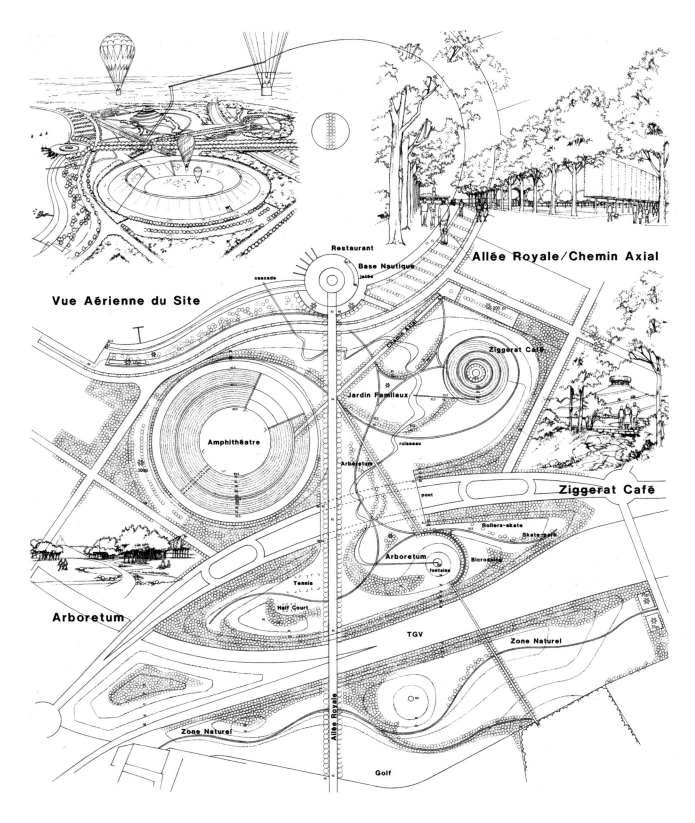

Vue Aërienne du Site

Restaurant

Base Nautique

cascade

Allée Royale/Chemin Axial

jetée

Chemin Axial

Ziggerat Café

Jardin Familaux

ruisseau

Amphithéatre

Arboretum

300pi

pont

Ziggerat Café

Rollers-skate

Skate-park

Arboretum

fontaine

Bicrossing

Tennis

Arboretum

Half Court

TGV

Zone Naturel

75pi

35pi

Zone Naturel

Allée Royale

Golf

Plan hand-drawn in ink on tracing paper and then coloured as shown opposite

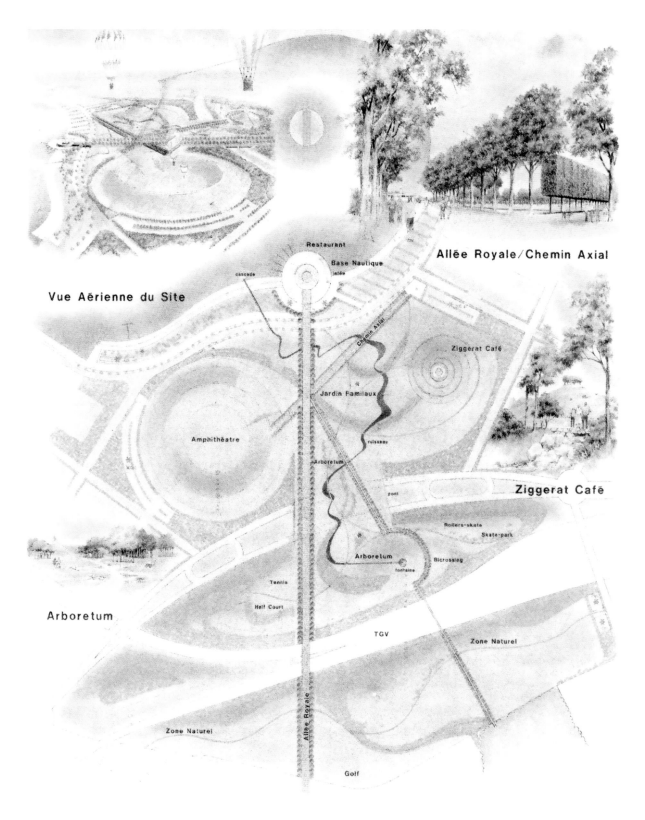

Vue Aērienne du Site

Allēe Royale/Chemin Axial

Ziggerat Café

Arboretum

Restaurant
Base Nautique
cascade
jetée
Chemin Axial
Ziggerat Café
Jardin Familaux
ruisseau
Arboretum
pont
Amphithéatre
Rollers-skate
Skate-park
Arboretum
Bicrossing
fontaine
Tennis
Half Court
TGV
Zone Naturel
Allée Royale
Zone Naturel
Golf

The competition plan is hand-drawn in ink on
tracing paper and a copy coloured with pastels

The Masterplan : Lac de Sénart, France

Chiron Diagnostics HQ
Suffolk

Chiron Diagnostics Headquarters, Sudbury, Suffolk

The patterns of the past revealed themselves subtly and became the inspiration for this contemporary landscape design

The largest Iron Age settlement in Suffolk had just been uncovered, with evidence of round houses, an enclosure ditch and a roadway. Saxon and early medieval traces, including a long straight trackway, were also found. Archaeologists were still at work, exposing layers of history which were all carefully recorded and then covered for future generations. This was my first site visit to two fields in Chilton, on the edge of Sudbury, that were to become the site of a new headquarters for Chiron Diagnostics.

The 33-acre site lies between Chilton Hall, a moated Tudor manor house and St Mary's Church. The fifteenth-century church is now isolated in the rural landscape, having lost its parish long ago. A green lane connects the two sites, slicing through rolling arable fields in a straight line. A stream drains three medieval ponds in Chilton Hall gardens and I was told that eels had swum up this water course for centuries. This was one of the richest historic landscapes, I had encountered. The patterns of the past revealed themselves subtly; this landscape was seamed with human stories.

The narrative for a new landscape was born out of the fragments of past activities. The design drew on the idea of three important building groups: the moated Manor House, St Mary's Church and the headquarters' campus, all lying at the edge of the archaeological area. The moat and medieval ponds at Chilton Hall, led to the idea that the new development was also on a moated island. Two causeways cross the moat to the headquarters' building, arriving at an entrance court. The water re-appears in the rear courtyard, almost as though it were a fragment of the moat. The roads and car park have been shaped to reflect the linear geometry of the trackways found in the historic landscape. Inspired by the Iron Age and medieval earthworks, the new landscape has been sculpted to create crisp landforms. The archaeological finds in the landscape will be marked by means of earth sculpting or planting to serve as memories of the passage of time.

A shelter belt of indigenous trees has been planted to screen the manor house and the church from the new development. A cycle path is located within the wooded edge. These are the only two elements of this scheme which were implemented.

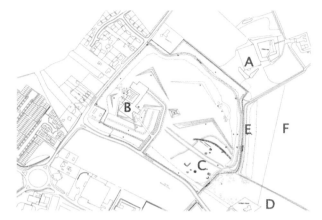

A Chilton Hall   D St Mary's Church
B Chiron HQ campus   E Green Lane
C Archaeological area   F Footpath

CREDITS

Client :
Chiron Diagnostics
Landscape Architects :
Armstrong Bell Landscape Design
Architects :
Kemp Muir Wealleans
Client Design Consultant :
Pocknell Studio
Date : 1997–2000

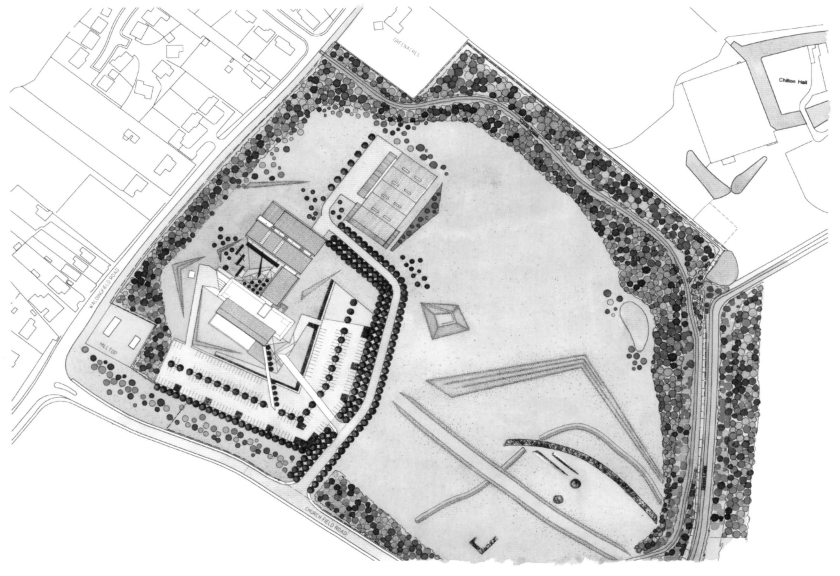

The headquarters' campus looks over the landscape with the
archaeological finds marked by earth sculpting and planting.
The moated Chilton Hall is visible top right.

The Masterplan : Chiron Diagnostics Headquarters, Suffolk

41

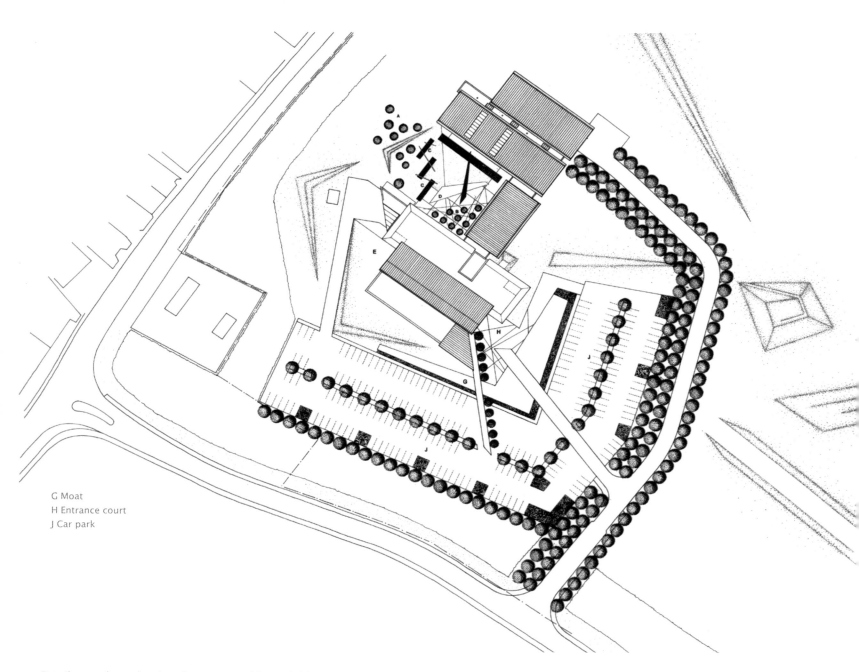

G Moat
H Entrance court
J Car park

Detail area plan : showing the campus with two bridges crossing
the moat, linking the car park to the entrance court

Plan hand-drawn in ink on tracing
paper with some collaged elements

View from the car park bridge towards the entrance court, with earth sculpting
inspired by the history of the site visible through the trees in the distance

The Moated Campus : Chiron Diagnostics Headquarters, Suffolk

Duke of York's Square
London

Duke of York's Square, King's Road, Chelsea, London

Dynamic and vibrant, this contemporary design reflects the history of the Kings Road as the home of trendsetting fashion and the creative arts

The design for this new public square reflects the vibrant nature and sartorial history of the Kings Road. Home to trendsetting fashion and the birth of social movements, from Mary Quant through to the Punks, the Kings Road has been a magnet for the creative arts.

One of four finalists in an ideas competition for Duke of York's Square, the design presents a dynamic and contemporary approach previously unseen in Chelsea. The square is the gateway to the retail area in Sloane Place and the design was required to visually connect the two.

A geometry of stone lines and wall-seats lead people into the site to experience the Glass Cube café, a water splash and lines of light in the paving. The stone paving is cut by lines of darker stone which express either movement or visual axes. A strong diagonal line leads the eye from the King's Road into the inner shopping court. Trees line this route to further emphasise its importance, whilst a water splash feature draws people into the space. A glass fence is proposed to the rear of the square to allow views into the green area beyond.

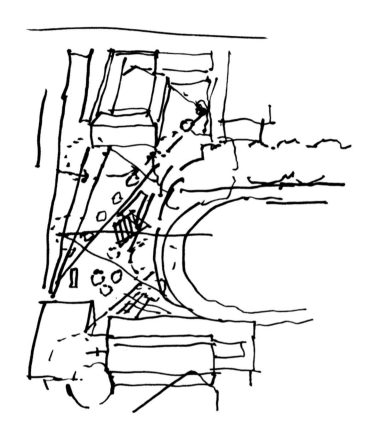

CREDITS
Client : Cadogan Estates
Architect : Paul Davis & Partners
Landscape Architect :
Armstrong Bell Landscape Design
Date : 1999

Development sketch showing a strong diagonal movement line with trees leading from the King's Road to the inner court. The Glass Cube Café is centrally placed against the backdrop of the green area to the rear.

Sketch showing the Glass Cube Café and the strong
diagonal band of paving which leads to the inner court

Design Development : Duke of York's Square, London

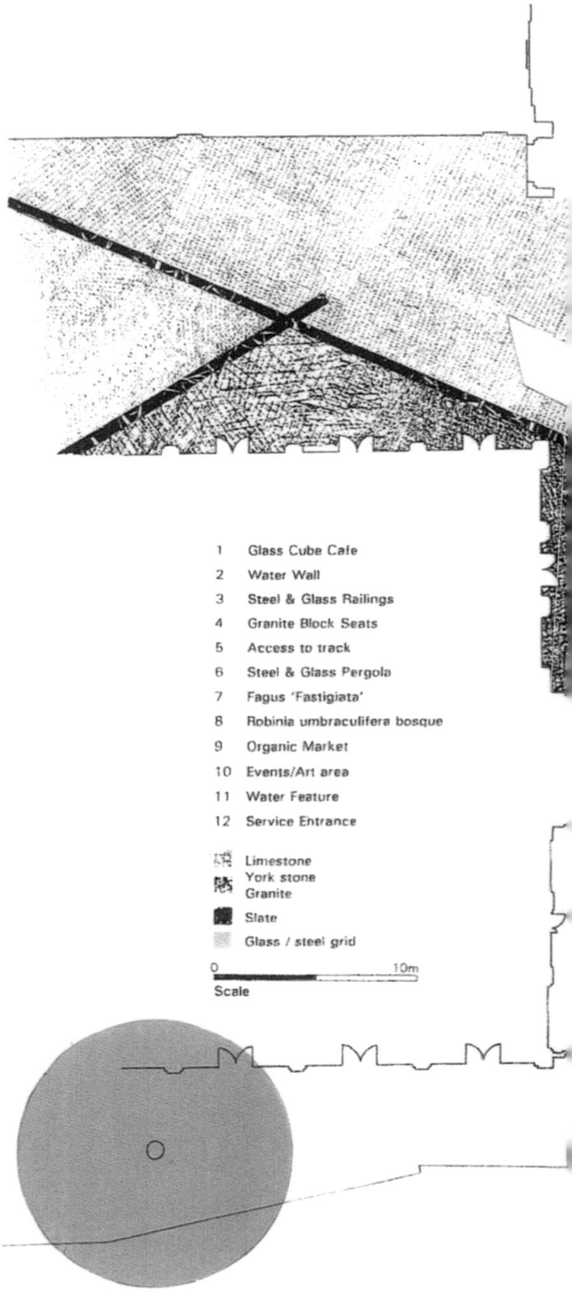

1 Glass Cube Cafe
2 Water Wall
3 Steel & Glass Railings
4 Granite Block Seats
5 Access to track
6 Steel & Glass Pergola
7 Fagus 'Fastigiata'
8 Robinia umbraculifera bosque
9 Organic Market
10 Events/Art area
11 Water Feature
12 Service Entrance

Limestone
York stone
Granite
Slate
Glass / steel grid

0   10m
Scale

This competition entry was hand-drawn in ink
on tracing paper with some collaged elements

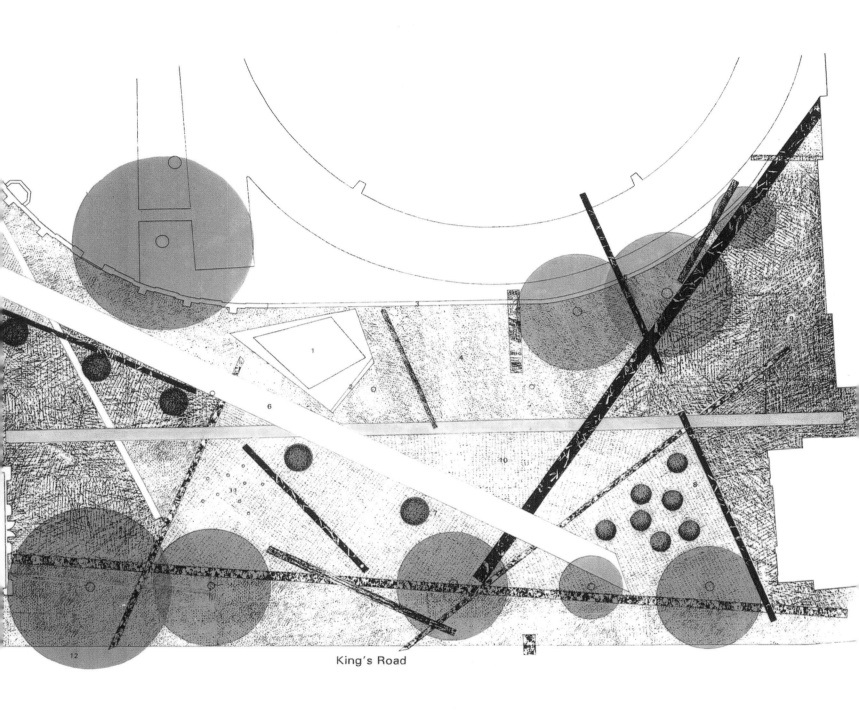

King's Road

The Design : Duke of York's Square, London

Visualisation : Duke of York's Square, London

Electra Park
London

Electra Park, West Ham, London

This contemporary piazza on the banks of Bow Creek is part of a jigsaw of green spaces which connect the River Thames to the Lea Valley Regional Park

Bow Creek is a place of big skies and long views downstream to the River Thames, towards the Millennium Dome. The tidal creek has a sense of the wild; it is a corridor for birds and people, part of a jigsaw of green spaces which connect the Lea Valley Regional Park via the Olympic Park, to the Thames.

The site was formerly West Ham power station, which was cleared, leaving the site contaminated and infested with Japanese knotweed. After a long process of remediation, the site was ready for a new life as an industrial park. The old wharf on the banks of Bow Creek, was to become a contemporary piazza and yet retain the ability to operate as a wharf if required. Silver clad units flank a central boulevard leading to the piazza.

The line of an old dock wall was discovered during excavations and this memory of former times has been marked by a low gabion wall which retains sweeping curves of ornamental grasses, studded with multi-stem birch and *Prunus serrula*. Sealed gravel paving cut by a blue glass line of recycled glass, a silver granite square and a bespoke bench in 'Orsogril' create an abstract geometry. Birch planted in galvanised planters are scattered across the piazza.

Leading out of the piazza heading northwards and edging the River Walk, indigenous planting provides cover for wildlife and screens the units from Bow Creek.

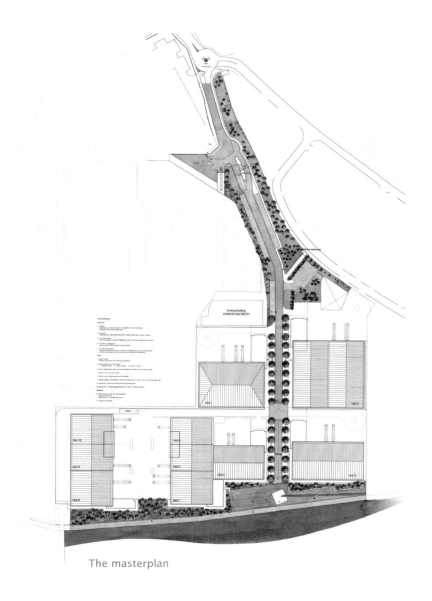

The masterplan

CREDITS
Client : Harbour Land
Landscape Architects : Armstrong Bell Landscape Design
Architects : Kemp Muir Wealleans
Consulting Engineers : Arup
Date : 2002

The piazza with the gabion wall on the right,
the blue glass line and the bespoke bench,
all arranged in an abstract geometry

The Masterplan and Piazza : Electra Park, London

The Piazza Design

The discovery of an old dock wall inspired the abstract arrangement of elements in the design, bringing new life to this historic wharf

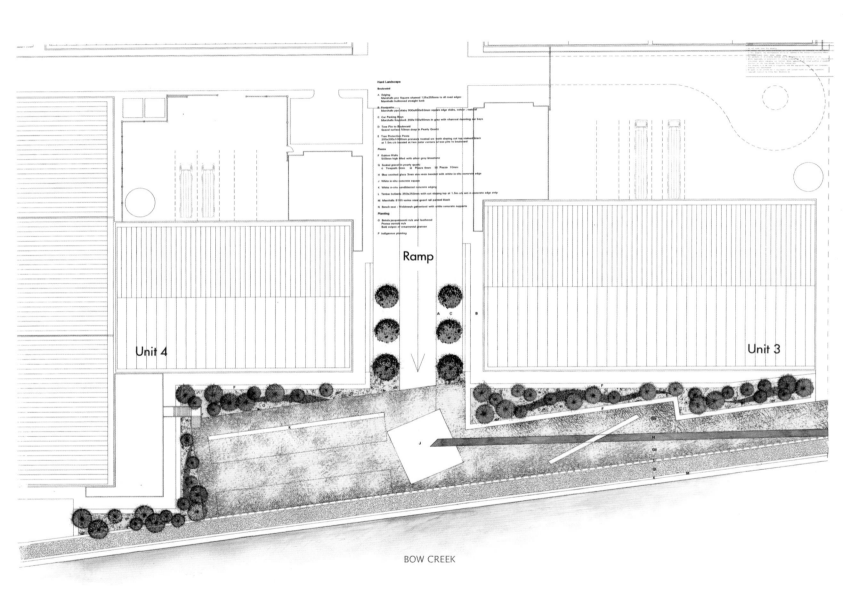

Ramp

Unit 4

Unit 3

BOW CREEK

Plan hand-drawn in ink on CAD baseplan

The disposition of a long bench, a blue line and the galvanised planters create an unusual aesthetic whilst native *Deschampsia* grasses held by a stone-filled gabion wall, edge the piazza.

The Piazza Design : Electra Park, London

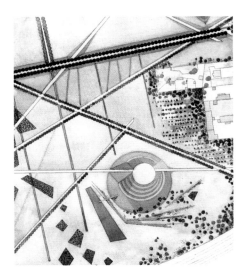

Parco Franco Verga
Milan, Italy

Parco Franco Verga, Milan, Italy

Formerly named Parco Certosa

Part of an ambitious plan to turn Milan green, the park lies at the heart of a new neighbourhood

PROGRAMME
Design completed 1997
Construction drawings completed 2000
Construction :
Phase 1 : northern part of site including raised walkway and canals completed 2006
Phase 2 : southern part of site with the exception of the amphitheatre and lake completed 2012

CREDITS
Client : Il Comune di Milano
Landscape Architects :
Armstrong Bell Landscape Design
Engineers : Arup
Architect (for kiosks) : Curzi & Sala
Perspective Artist : Richard Carman
Mural Artist : TV Boy
Photography : Milano Panoramica and Diana Armstrong Bell

Milan is at the heart of European design and fashion, a busy and vibrant city that feels fast moving. Buildings in the centre are grand and up-scaled, reflecting Milan's place as the commercial hub of Italy. Yet, Milan had few green spaces and little tradition of local public parks, until the Comune di Milano prepared an ambitious plan to turn Milan green.

'Nove Parchi per Milano' was duly published in 1995, a planning document intended as a brief for the creation of nine new parks for the city. Further to an international portfolio competition, five landscape architects – Diana Armstrong Bell, Peter Latz, Michel Desvigne, Christophe Girot and Guido Ferrara – were selected and each allocated a park to design in 1997.

I was invited to design Parco Franco Verga, a 23-ha site in Quarto Oggiaro, northern Milan. The park was intended as the focus of a new neighbourhood being developed by EuroMilano, with a commercial centre and station to the west. New housing was designed to border the park on three sides whilst the railway line forms the southern boundary. The new university campus of Bovisa lies to the south of the railway line.

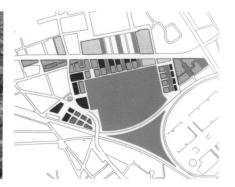

Right : aerial view of the site before remediation, with blue storage tanks of the oil refinery visible
Far right : zoning diagram, the park is shown as a green square

The park at night
Image : Milano Panoramica

Parco Franco Verga, Milan

The Site

A cherry tree, laden with blossom, seemed to represent former times when the site was green

The first site visit revealed an area which had been despoiled by industry; an oil refinery had left the site contaminated and in need of remediation and cleaning before any new design could be implemented. A feeling of abandonment prevailed, leaving people in the social housing to the north of the site nowhere to relax, play or just enjoy being in the open air.

There was little trace of the site's history as agricultural land except two dried-up streams, which suggested that cultivated fields had once inhabited this place. Bordering the east side of the site, via Porretta is a tiny enclave of houses along a cobbled street, with well tended gardens and allotments. It appeared oddly isolated in the urban decay, a patch of green in a grey landscape. A solitary cherry tree, laden with blossom, hung down over the grey soil. It seemed to represent a fragment of a former time when the site was green.

This page
Aerial view of the site
Opposite
Top left : via Porretta
Top right : solitary cherry tree
Bottom : the site with social housing to the rear

THE SITE

The Site : Parco Franco Verga, Milan

Site Context

This idea of gathering fragments of a site's history took hold as a source of inspiration for the design

Considering what the site might once have been like led to an exploration of the Lombardy countryside. The paddy fields south of Milan are a surprising sight with their geometry of wet squares divided by raised earth banks, which seem to stretch to the horizon. This is overlaid by a separate geometry of poplar trees, planted in tight grids which appear as blocks of green. Occasional frail lines of trees edge the paddy fields, adding a delicate quality to this bold landscape.

Water has played a crucial role in the history of Milan. The geology of the area allows spring lines to occur, creating a seeming abundance of water in this flat landscape. The historic map of Milan of 1832 (see opposite), shows the old city encircled by canals.

These were used to bring food and supplies into the city. In the 1920s and 30s a programme of filling in and covering the canals and converting the spaces to roads changed the whole feeling of the city. Today, only a couple of canals exist, including Naviglio Grande and Milan feels disconnected with its watery past.

This drilling down to understand the landscape, its geology, history, memories, what once happened there and how it feels, is a crucial part of the design process. It means spending time in a landscape, observing, listening and gathering clues to inform a new story. This is especially the case for brown field sites which may at first appear devoid of clues, a blank canvas. But the land is never blank, it is up to us as designers to find its story. and connect a landscape back into its context.

Paddy fields south of Milan

Naviglio Grande

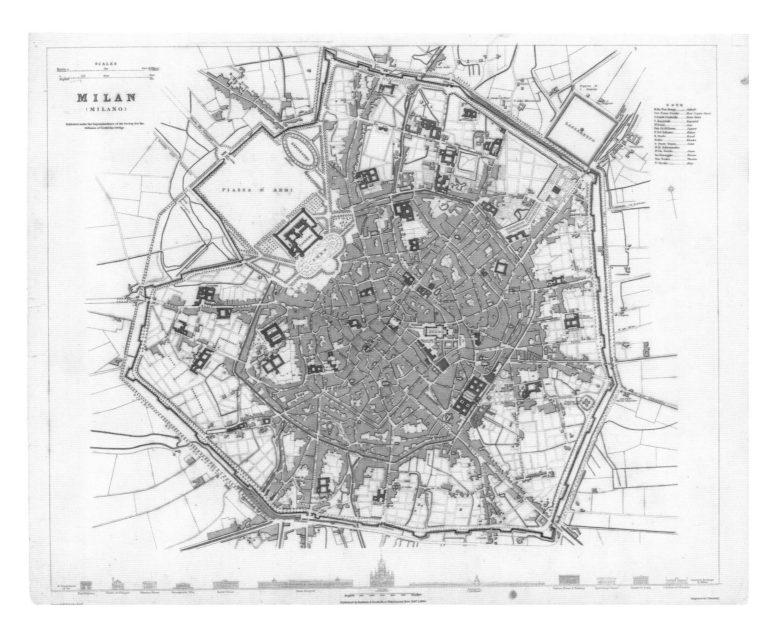

Historic map of Milan 1832 showing the city encircled by canals

Milan as a city of water : Context : Parco Franco Verga, Milan

Site Analysis Abstracts

Diagrams showing all aspects of the site and its context that led to a design strategy

SITE ACCESS

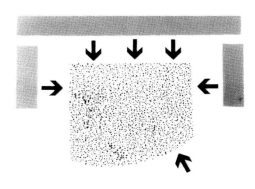

- Identify pedestrian entrances to the park
- Allow permeability for residents
- Site car parks at main entrances

VISUAL AXES

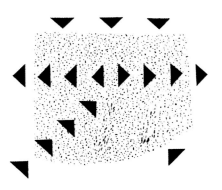

- Identify visual / movement axes into and out of the park
- Use these axes to develop a path system

HISTORY OF THE SITE

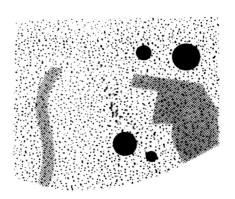

- Isolated fragments of a former landscape abandoned in the urban decay
- An old village street marooned in the waste
- A solitary cherry tree blossoms, a sign of hope for a renewed landscape
- A dried-up stream signals a past story

MILAN : CITY AND PORT

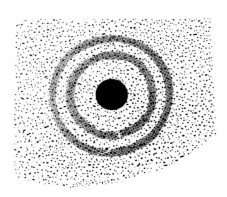

- Historic Milan was encircled by canals; the city was once a port

All drawings by hand in collage and ink on tracing paper

GEOLOGY

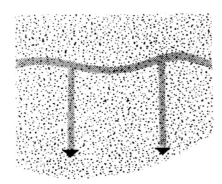

- The geology gives rise to springs

RURAL LOMBARDY

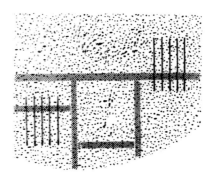

- A geometry of flooded paddy fields divided by raised earth embankments
- Grids of poplar trees create green sculpture in a flat landscape

LANDSCAPE STRATEGY 1

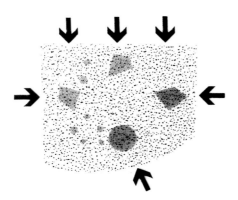

- Piazzas are situated at the three main entrances to attract people into the park
- 'Fragment Gardens' are inspired by the flowering cherry tree of via Porretta

LANDSCAPE STRATEGY 2

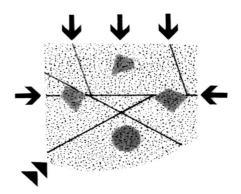

- Visual axes define a strong path system
- The design responds to the story of water in Milan and Lombardy
- The green amphitheatre is a visual focus

Site Analysis Abstracts : Parco Franco Verga, Milan

The Design

Inspired by the history and memories of the site and its context, the design uses earth modelling and water to create a new story for this landscape

The structural framework of the park has been developed further to study of the visual and directional axes which link the park with the neighbourhood. These axes have been used to make a path network of strong lines which create an abstract geometry. Entrances have been positioned in response to transport links and local pedestrian movement. A piazza with a café/kiosk with integral public WC has been sited at each of the three main entrances to draw people into the park and as a means of creating supervised active spaces.

The history of Milan as a port and the landscape of rural Lombardy led to the use of water and earth modelling in the design. A raised earth walkway, 2.5-3m high, crowned with an avenue of trees, is reminiscent of the embankments seen in the paddy fields of rural Lombardy. The walkway marches across the site in a straight line from east to west, connecting two main entrances. Piazza Ovest (west) is at ground level at one end, Piazza Est (east) is at the other end, at the high level of the walkway, with views down over the park. Paths slope up to meet the raised earth walkway, adding a further layer of interest as the earth slopes and tilts, to accommodate changes in level. Water pours from the southern bank of the walkway to feed four canals which run due south towards the railway line.

The main route out of Milan heading north, passes the west side of the site, elevated on stilts, allowing views across the park where the visual focus was designed to be a sculptural earth amphitheatre associated with a lake fed by a concrete water wall. This whole relationship of elements would be seen against a backdrop of trees. This area was designed as a cultural hub which would relate to the new Universtity at Bovisa, at the other side of the railway line. Architects Curzi & Sala designed a restaurant building which slotted into the amphitheatre.

At the time of writing this book, the amphitheatre, restaurant, lake and water wall have not been implemented, leaving the southern part of the site without its intended purpose. It is to be hoped that funds will yet be found to complete this important part of the design.

In the foreground a series of 'Fragment Gardens', inspired by the solitary cherry tree of via Porretta, appear as though scattered across the planes of grass, a drift of colour against the green. Each garden is richly planted and enclosed with hedges, an intimate space in contrast to the open grass areas.

Ball games areas and play areas lie to the north of the raised earth walkway, adjacent to the new housing. Grids of poplar trees are planted along the western boundary in bold groups to screen the park from built-up areas beyond. Allotments border via Porretta, enhancing the village character whilst indigenous tree planting edges the whole park.

The Influence of Abstract Art on the Design

The influence of the artist Malevich can be seen in the design drawings which follow, where earth is sculpted and designed elements are placed to create a geometry which does not draw reference from classical precedents. The first design drawing was a simple collage where all the elements, piazzas, paths, etc, were represented by loose paper cut-outs which remained mobile until they were arranged in a satisfactory series of relationships. Testing what happens when an element is moved and looking closely at the spaces between objects eventually results in a design which appears to have a dynamic which is at variance with more traditional ways of designing space. When the collage is considered fixed, the design is then drawn in ink on tracing paper.

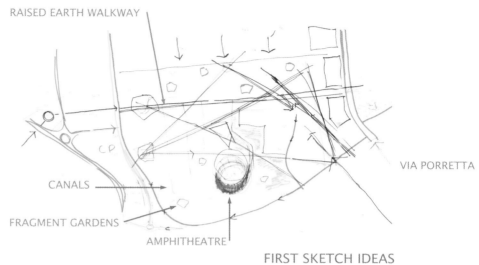

ACCESS FROM HOUSING AREA

RAISED EARTH WALKWAY

VIA PORRETTA

CANALS

FRAGMENT GARDENS

AMPHITHEATRE

FIRST SKETCH IDEAS

Felt pen and crayon on tracing paper

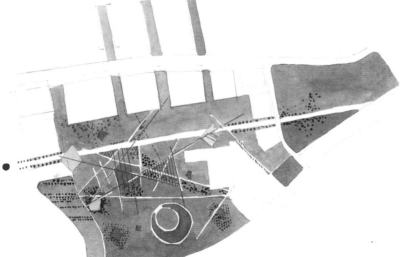

DEVELOPMENT SKETCH PLAN

Drawn in pencil and watercolour

IDEAS FOR RAISED WALKWAY AND CANALS

Sketch Design : Parco Franco Verga, Milan

The green amphitheatre and a lake fed by a concrete water wall are the visual focus for the southern part of the park. The canals and 'Fragment Gardens', shown in red, are all viewed against a backdrop of trees.

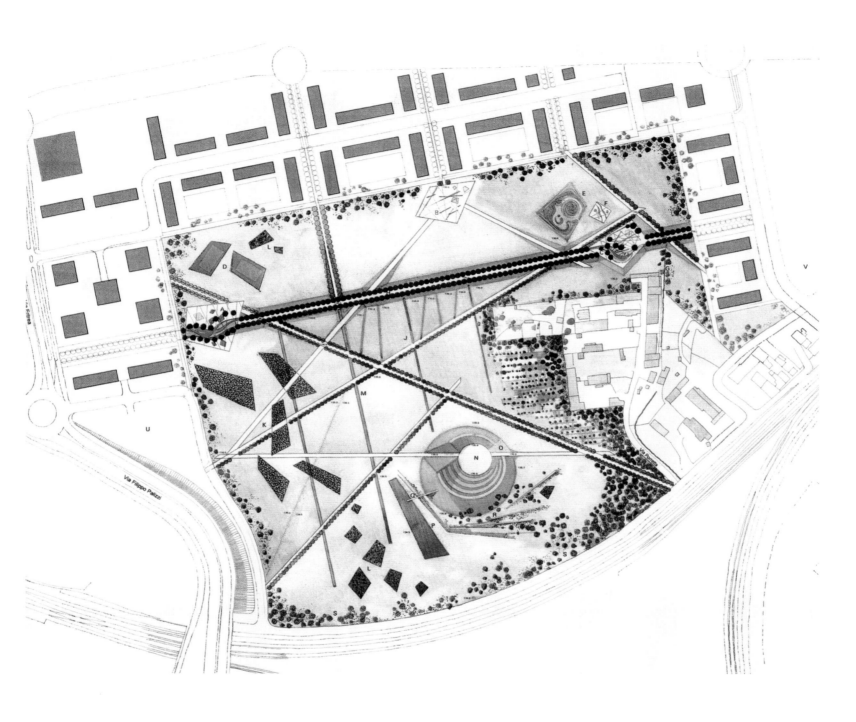

A Piazza Ovest
B Piazza Nord
C Piazza Est
D Ball games courts
E Sculptural play area
F Play area : infants
G Stream

H Raised earth walkway
J Sculpted planes of earth
K Grids of poplar trees
L Fragment Gardens
M Canals
N Green amphitheatre
O Café / services

P Lake
Q Concrete water wall
R Amphitheatre gardens
S Ecological planting
T Allotments and wood
U Car park
V Provisional car park

Exhibited at the Royal Academy, Summer Exhibition 2019

Hand-drawn in ink on tracing paper,
copied and watercoloured

Green Amphitheatre and The Masterplan : Parco Franco Verga, Milan

Panorama over the park from Piazza Ovest
with the ball games areas in the foreground

Image : Milano Panoramica

Panorama : Parco Franco Verga, Milan

Water pours from the banks of the raised earth walkway to feed four canals. The earth slopes and tilts as paths rise up to meet the walkway.

The park in winter... a woman and her dog
walk up to the raised earth walkway, with one
of the canals visible in the distance

Image : Milano Panoramica

Raised Earth Walkway and Canals : Parco Franco Verga, Milan

Grids of poplar trees inspired by those seen in the Lombardy landscape are scattered along the west side of the park, screening the built-up areas beyond

Image : Milano Panoramica

Panorama over the park from Piazza Ovest in the foreground. Grids of poplar trees are seen on the right, and the raised earth walkway crosses the park towards the high buildings in the distance. This early evening photograph captures the shadows created by the paths as they rise out of the ground to slope up to the higher level of the walkway.

Image : Milano Panoramica

Grids of Poplar Trees and Raised Earth Walkway : Parco Franco Verga, Milan

The Three Piazzas

A fragmented geometry of granite paving with water, trees and earth embankments derive from the design concepts developed for the park as a whole

Introduction

A piazza with a café/kiosk has been situated at each of the three main entrances to attract people into the park. Piazza Nord is the main entrance into the park from the new residential area and the social housing which lies beyond. Piazza Ovest is at ground level at the western end of the raised earth walkway, close to a residential area and the commercial centre and station. Piazza Est lies at the eastern extremity of the raised earth walkway and at the same elevated level, giving views down over the park.

The design concepts developed for the park as a whole, have been used in each piazza. The idea of Milan as a city of water, coupled with the curious geology which produces unexpected spring lines, have been used to develop a relationship of paving and water in each piazza. The strong lines, water features, earth embankments and plantations of poplar trees are all inspired by the Lombardy landscape. The lone flowering cherry tree of via Porretta, which holds the memory of the site in greener times, led to the planting of cherry trees in Piazza Nord. All three piazzas are variations on a theme of the design concept and each share the same kiosk design. Piazza Nord is described in some detail.

Piazza Nord

Sculpted grass embankments define and contain the piazza, which is paved with a fragmented geometry of black granite lines in a background of light grey granite.

Low concrete walls running north to south on both sides of the piazza define the granite area and create a step up to terraces surfaced in gravel and planted with trees. On the western side, a water channel is set into the top of a low concrete wall which runs the entire length of the piazza. A line of blue/green glass paving at the base of the wall acts almost as a reflection of the water channel above. Lombardy poplar trees are planted on this terrace to provide shade and a sense of enclosure. On the eastern side of the piazza two terraces are retained by low concrete walls which act as both seats and steps. These terraces are planted with a grove of semi-mature cherry trees in varying sizes, creating the feeling of an old orchard. The central focus of the piazza is a concrete cube kiosk with rooftop seating, a water wall and a stainless steel pergola. The three elements are placed in a composition, allowing interesting views into and through the piazza across the angled lines in the paving. The pergola has a sculptural quality where all the cross members set into the 'roof' are placed at slightly different angles, giving the feeling of a spine in movement. The kiosk, designed as a café coupled with public services, was originally in unpainted concrete but subsequently murals have been added by TV Boy. The kiosks which serve drinks and snacks are an important part of the strategy for 'policing' the park by means of creating active supervised spaces. Piazza Nord is now very well used by local residents and dog walkers who appear to enjoy the water features and shady terraces.

This early concept drawing shows ideas for the three piazzas. Milan as a city of water, the poplar trees and earth sculpting found in the Lombardy landscape have been reinterpreted to create designs which reference concepts used in the design of the park as a whole.

The Piazzas : Parco Franco Verga, Milan

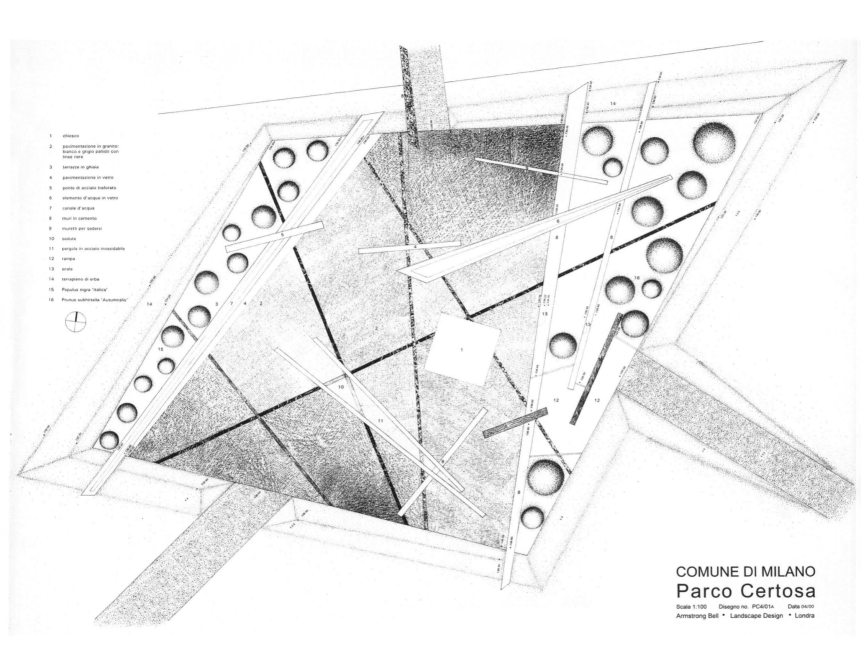

1   chiosco
2   pavimentazione in granito:
    bianco e grigio pallido con
    linee nere
3   terrazze in ghiaia
4   pavimentazione in vetro
5   ponte di acciaio traforato
6   elemento d'acqua in vetro
7   canale d'acqua
8   muri in cemento
9   muretti per sedersi
10 sedute
11 pergola in acciaio inossidabile
12 rampa
13 scala
14 terrapieno di erba
15 Populus nigra 'Italica'
16 Prunus subhirtella 'Autumnalis'

COMUNE DI MILANO
Parco Certosa
Scala 1:100   Disegno no. PC4/01A   Data 04/00
Armstrong Bell • Landscape Design • Londra

The presentation drawing for Piazza Nord, with its original name, Parco Certosa. The concrete cube kiosk is flanked by a water wall and a pergola. The terraces with trees are shown on the right and left of the space. A water channel runs along the left hand side of the paving, set into the top of a low wall.

Hand-drawn in ink on tracing paper, some textures are applied by collage

Visualisation of the piazza showing the water wall, pergola
and water channel with Lombardy poplars on the right

Piazza Nord : Parco Franco Verga, Milan

Top left : water channel set in top of wall and poplars
Top right : stainless steel pergola with stone seat
Bottom left : view from steps leading to roof terrace
Bottom right : concrete cube kiosk as designed and
before murals were added later by the client

Images : Diana Armstrong Bell

Panorama over the park towards Piazza Ovest. The raised earth walkway is shown leading to the new flats in the distance. The four canals are just visible to the left of the walkway. Piazza Nord can be seen lower right.

Piazza Nord : Parco Franco Verga, Milan

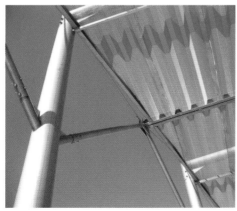

Above : panorama looking down at Piazza Est, with
the play area at a lower level in the background

Image : Milano Panoramica

Opposite : Piazza Est with concrete cube kiosk,
pergola, water splash and wave seat. Poplar trees
frame the space and create shade

Images : Diana Armstrong Bell

Piazza Est : Parco Franco Verga, Milan

The Play Area

Conceived as a land sculpture, where the earth is moulded and folded to create a landform that could become anything a child imagines

The play area is a curving and gently contoured space, a landform that was first modelled by hand to test ideas and shapes. The intention was to create a space which is interesting and provocative to a child's imagination rather than providing standard play equipment.

A water splash draws children into the space, which is carpeted in rubber paving with a composition of abstract lines. Murals by TV Boy, painted on to the walls of a study centre/kiosk form a lively backdrop to the water splash. The murals were not part of the original design but added subsequently by the client. A series of low concrete walls curve around the water feature, each one a step, retaining a change in level which leads up to the grassed embankments, which enclose the whole area. An apple orchard on the grassy slopes, provides shady places to sit and picnic. Two main sculptural elements are placed at either side of the entrance, on elevated land. The ziggurat is an earth formation, 2–3 metres high with a spiral path to the top. Encircled by a series of curving walls, it has the feeling of a fortification. One of these walls is topped with a mosaic in an abstract pattern which could represent a dragon, a river or whatever a child might imagine. The kaleidoscope hill is a curious circular mound with an entrance at either side, leading into a child-sized room lined with mirror mosaic. Coloured glass covers a hole in the roof, allowing the sun to create kaleidoscopic patterns in the mosaic.

The study centre and kiosks were not opened for several years after the park was built, which led to a lack of supervision in the park and an absence of services. As a result, the council closed the kaleidoscope hill which is a sad loss of an unusual feature.

The People Make the Park Their Own

One hot summer's day, a few years after completion of the park, I spent a day there, just observing how it was being used. The play area was a honeypot of activity, well used by local residents, who regard the water splash as their own beach. People come for the day with picnics and towels almost as though they were going to the seaside. One boy said, 'We can't afford to go to the beach, this is our beach, we love it, we love the park!'

Sketch model to test initial ideas in the studio that developed into the final plan shown opposite

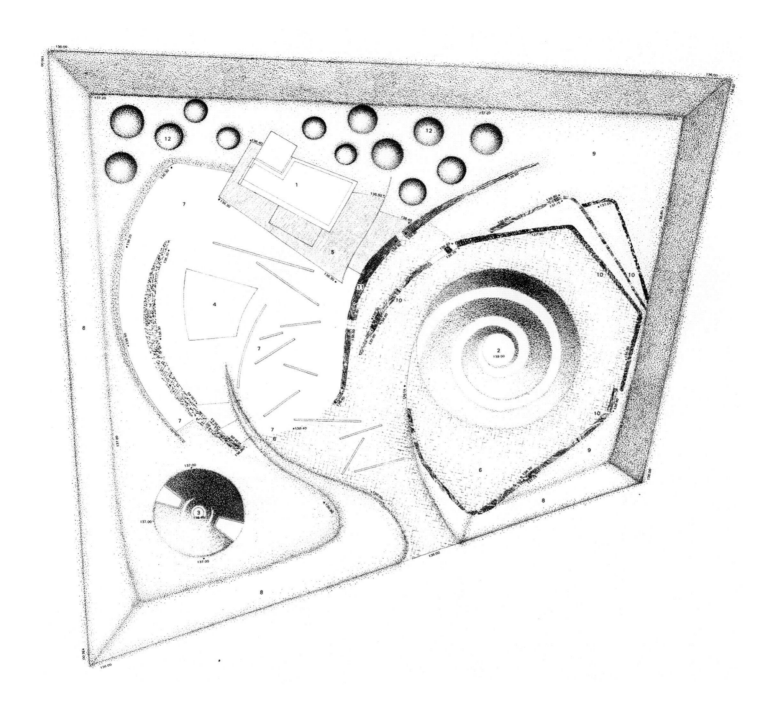

1 Study centre
2 Ziggurat
3 Kaleidoscope hill
4 Water splash

The ziggurat on the right and the kaleidoscope hill on the left, frame the entrance to the play area. A series of low walls curve around the study centre to the rear and an apple orchard is planted on the grassy bank.

Plan hand-drawn in Ink on tracing paper with some collaged elements

Play Area Plan : Parco Franco Verga, Milan

Top : rubber play surface with the kaleidoscope hill and raised earth walkway to the rear

Opposite top : the ziggurat with the kaleidoscope hill in the background and mosaic-topped wall on the right

Opposite bottom : a shady picnic in the apple orchard and the water splash becomes a beach with a backdrop of murals by TV Boy

Images : Diana Armstrong Bell

Play Area : Parco Franco Verga, Milan

Panorama looking down at the play area with Piazza
Nord in the background and the new housing beyond

Image : Milano Panoramica

Play Area : Parco Franco Verga, Milan

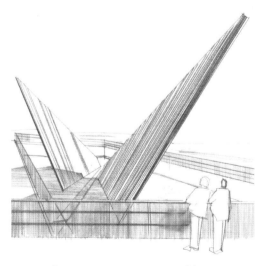

Sculpture Installation
London

Sculpture Installation, Canary Wharf, London

Competition-winning designs for this former dock drew inspiration from the idea of flowing water, creating movement, rhythm and change

The Site

A temporary landscape was required for this concrete-lined basement which was to be the footprint of a future building near One Canada Square. The ramp to an underground car park slices through the concrete basement, bisecting it in half. One half is 6 m below general footpath level and the other is just over 2 m below. These lower areas are contained by vertical concrete walls. A covered concrete truck ramp contains one side of the deepest space and offers a blank wall towards the site. This arrangement of concrete, horizontal and vertical planes cut by angled ramps makes a strong composition of elements, which in itself has abstract qualities. The site is overlooked from adjacent paths on three sides and looked down on from surrounding tall buildings.

The Design

Discovering the history of a place, unearthing its story, is my starting point for landscape design projects. This site was once a dock, a place of activity, movement and water, and the design uses this idea to create a new life for this curious place.

The design process started by making two site models in foam board, one for each option. Then a series of fins were cut out and moved around in the space to gauge the effect when viewed from above and when moving round the site. It seemed essential that the elements within the design should rise out of the deep and be visible to people at pavement level. Each fin was pinned in place when the elements were working together. Plans were drawn only when three-dimensional issues were resolved on the models. Development sketches and perspectives were also drawn using the models.

Option One

Three stainless steel fins emerge from the ground plane, creating a composition in which the physical form of the site plays a part. The fins appear as finely honed objects rising from the rugged texture of the concrete basement. From pavement level, the sculpture can be viewed from three sides. Moving round the site the fins can be seen in a serially changing relationship to one another, creating a sensation of movement. Viewed from the buildings above, the perspective is different again. Each fin is leaning, creating tension between the three objects, whilst the car ramp becomes part of the composition of elements.

The ground is covered with white river cobbles cut by a blue line, which slides between two smaller fins, in memory of the previous presence of water. The red line placed on the side wall of the truck ramp is set with white LED lights, creating a star-like effect on the red surface.

By day, sun falling on the fins creates bold shadows, which move throughout the day, creating another layer of pattern. By night, a dramatic dimension is added when the three fins are illuminated by uplighters, effectively blacking out the main body of the site.

Option Two

This design follows the same principles as the first option but has a more lively and diverse composition of elements. Two stainless steel fins, two red fabric-covered fins and a vertical frame set with LED lights create mobility and tension in the way they are juxtaposed. The ground is covered with silvery, crushed CDs cut by a blue line in memory of the former prescence of water.

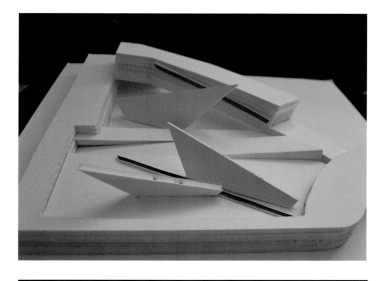
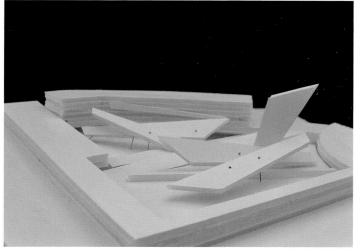
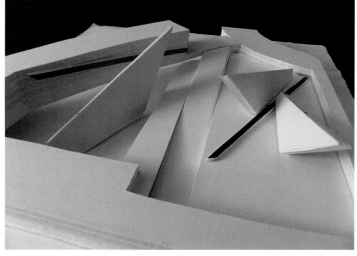
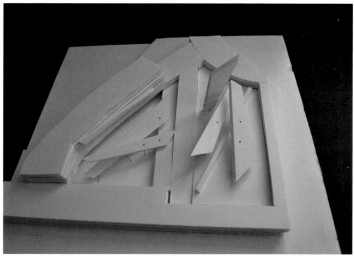

OPTION ONE

OPTION TWO

CREDITS
Client : Canary Wharf Group
Landscape Architects :
Armstrong Bell Landscape Design
Date : 2003

Sketch Models : Sculpture Installation, London

Moving round the site, the stainless steel fins can be seen in a
serially changing relationship, creating a sensation of movement

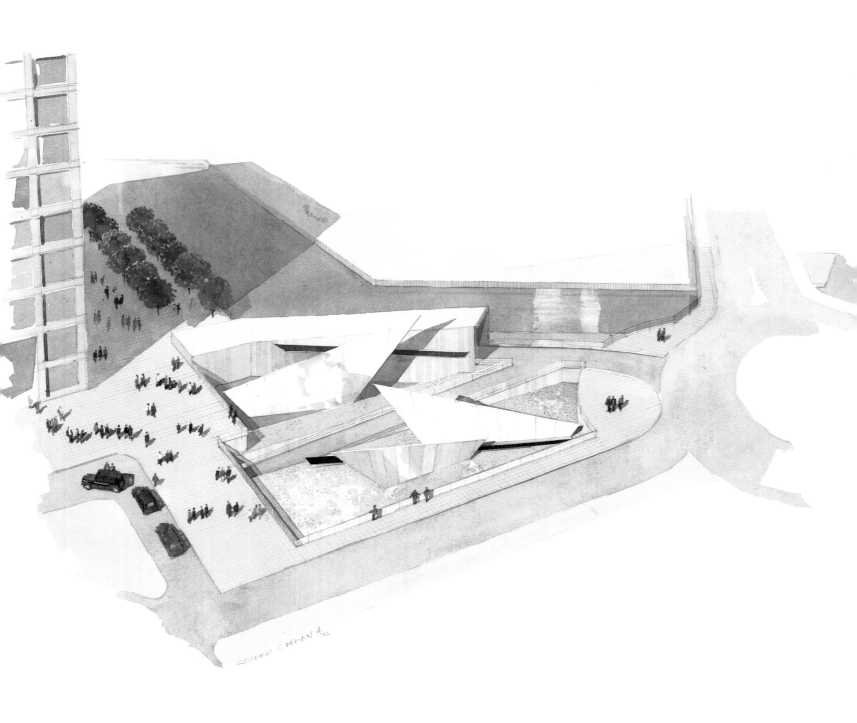

Option 1 : Sculpture Installation, London

RICHARD CARMAN '03

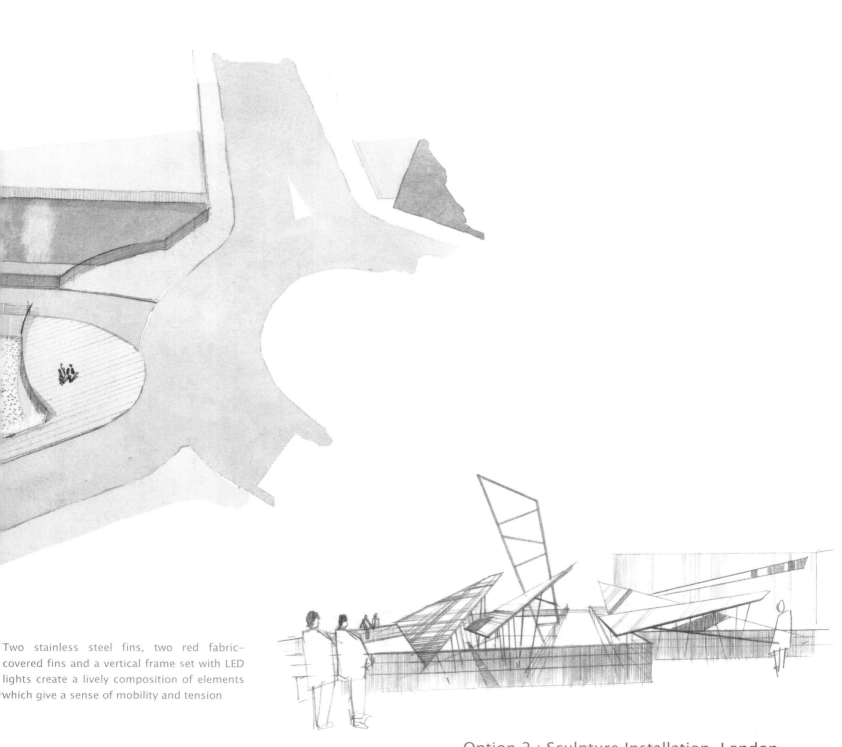

Two stainless steel fins, two red fabric-covered fins and a vertical frame set with LED lights create a lively composition of elements which give a sense of mobility and tension

Option 2 : Sculpture Installation, London

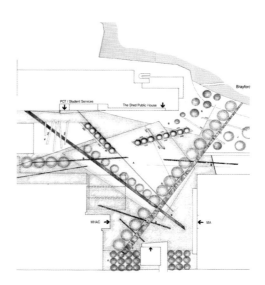

University of Lincoln
Brayford Pool Campus

University of Lincoln

Brayford Pool Campus Landscape Masterplan

The view across Brayford Pool to Lincoln Castle and Cathedral is one of the most celebrated picturesque views in Britain

The University of Lincoln is developing a contemporary campus at Brayford Pool with the celebration of these iconic vision lines at the heart of the project.

Our landscape masterplan for the 20-ha university campus was won in design competition but has not been implemented. Based on an architectural masterplan by Rick Mather Architects and co-ordinated by the University of Lincoln Architects, our design focussed on a central green park, linked by pedestrian routes to a series of piazzas, which allow free-flow between the city and the campus.

The site was once fenland, on the banks of Brayford Pool and the River Witham, and is overlaid by a web of history from the Celts through to the Romans and then the Victorians who built the railway line, which runs through the site, and an engine shed. Part of Rick Mather's masterplan had been implemented at the time of the competition. The historic engine shed had been renovated by UL Architects, for re-use and Rick Mather had built an AMC building which addressed a flat grassed area, which was to be the site of the new park. The Delf Lake, a balancing lake to alleviate flooding, lies within the green area. At the time of the competition, the site was in a state of partial abandonment and had become a refuge for a diversity of wildlife and flora.

Top : Lincoln Cathedral from Brayford Pool by John Bangay (1984)
Bottom : aerial view of the campus with Brayford Pool on the right
Opposite : architectural block plan by Rick Mather and UL Architects

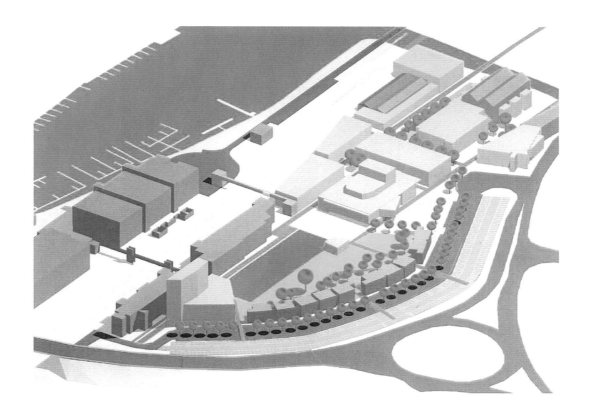

CREDITS
Client : University of Lincoln
Architects : Rick Mather and UL Architects
Landscape Architects : Armstrong Bell Landscape Design
Date : 2004-08

Introduction : Landscape Masterplan, University of Lincoln

The Fens

The curious qualities of the Lincolnshire landscape inspired the design ... the pattern was a perfect chequerboard reminiscent of a Mondrian painting

A journey by train, on my first visit to Lincoln, revealed the unusual qualities of the Lincolnshire landscape. In the winter sun, the land appeared cut by a latticework of straight channels, reflective and mirror-like. Fields were soot black, the alluvial soil fine and with the texture of softest suede. The overall pattern was a perfect man-made chequerboard, reminiscent of a Mondrian painting. Straight lines of trees occasionally broke the flatness. Roads, long and straight, sliced through the picture, raised on embankments, lifted above this watery landscape.

The images opposite illustrate the idea of landscape seen as a composition of line, form, colour and shadow, almost an abstraction of its purpose ... when landscape becomes art.

The Lincolnshire countryside is one of curious contrasts. The Fens lie to the east of a limestone escarpment, known as the Lincoln Edge, which runs in a straight, sharp line from north to south of the county. Lincoln is built on the escarpment, with its castle and cathedral seeming to hover over all they surround. Ermine Street, a Roman road, runs parallel to the escarpment, creating a landscape of linearity. This quality, coupled with the contrast between flatlands and escarpments, inspired the ideas for the competition.

Opposite top : At Welney. Kite aerial photography by Bill Blake Heritage Documentation
Opposite bottom : aerial view of the Lincolnshire Fens

The Fens : Landscape Masterplan, University of Lincoln

The Design

The image of the Lincolnshire landscape, coupled with vision and movement lines through the campus, translated into an unusual design concept

JMW Turner, along with many other artists, painted the picturesque view across Brayford Pool to Lincoln Cathedral and Castle. One of the key objectives of the design is to preserve this view, glimpsed between buildings from the central green space.

A third important visual axis is the view from the main site entrance to Delf Lake in the Central Green Space. These three axes, along with the movement lines between faculty buildings, form the structural framework of the design. The Central Green Space with the Delf Lake is the main focus of the landscape, with the Arts Square and River Square connected by means of a path system.

The masterplan design draws inspiration from the unusual quality of the Lincolnshire countryside. The landscape of the Fens with its flat fields cut by straight lines and crisp earth embankments, all viewed against the backdrop of the Lincoln Edge, influenced the landforms in the Central Green Space.

River Square

River Square is designed to mirror the robust scale of the adjacent old industrial buildings. A new timber bridge spans the river, linking the town with the campus. A line of light set in the paving travels from the bridge to the western end of the Square. A galvanised pergola structure composed of large-scale industrial RSJ-type members is set at an angle across the square, embracing a performance space and backed by a birch plantation. A third sculpture in Core-ten steel provides a focal point at the end of the Square. The pergola can be used to hang banners, sails and fabric backdrops for performances. A number of freestanding wall-seats appear as though scattered across the space.

Central Green Space and Delf Lake

Careful manipulation of line and form, has been used in this design to create an abstraction of the Lincolnshire landscape for the new park, with the Delf Lake as the central focus. An axial path slices through the space, crossing the lake on line with views to the castle and cathedral beyond. The path marking the visual axis from the main entrance in Rope Walk to the Delf Lake terminates in a sculptural gazebo composed of three Core-ten steel fragments, which rise from the lake. Sculpted earth forms held by a limestone gabion wall, derive from the memory of the Lincolnshire landscape. Cutting through the gabion, a stepped concrete water channel terminates in the lake with a water splash on axis with the gazebo. Flanking the Arts Centre, a grass pyramid offers seating for outdoor performances.

The design proposes aesthetic treatment to the Delf Lake without altering its function as a flood defence. Large concrete blocks are placed as random seat/steps leading down to the water's edge with indigenous planting between them. A plantation of native trees shelters the park from the road and adds to the sense of connection with the Lincolnshire countryside.

River Square

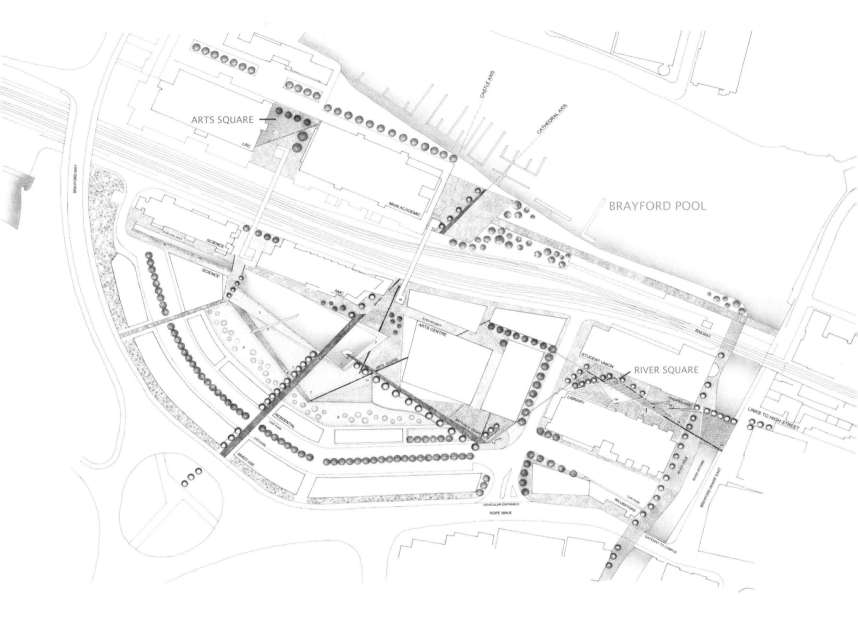

ARTS SQUARE

CASTLE AXIS

CATHEDRAL AXIS

BRAYFORD POOL

BRAYFORD WAY

LRC

MAIN ACADEMIC

SCIENCE

SCIENCE

AMC

ARTS CENTRE

RAILWAY

STUDENT UNION

RIVER SQUARE

LIBRARY

LINKS TO HIGH STREET

RESIDENTIAL

CAR PARK

MIXED USE

CAR PARK

VEHICULAR ENTRANCE

ROPE WALK

INCUBATORS

CAR PARK

GATEWAY TO CAMPUS

Section Through Central Green Space and Delf Lake

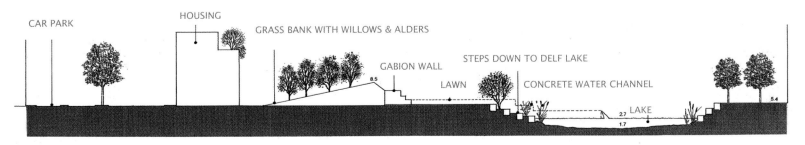

CAR PARK

HOUSING

GRASS BANK WITH WILLOWS & ALDERS

STEPS DOWN TO DELF LAKE

GABION WALL

LAWN

CONCRETE WATER CHANNEL

8.5

LAKE

2.7

1.7

5.4

Plan and section drawn
in ink on tracing paper

The Design : Landscape Masterplan, University of Lincoln

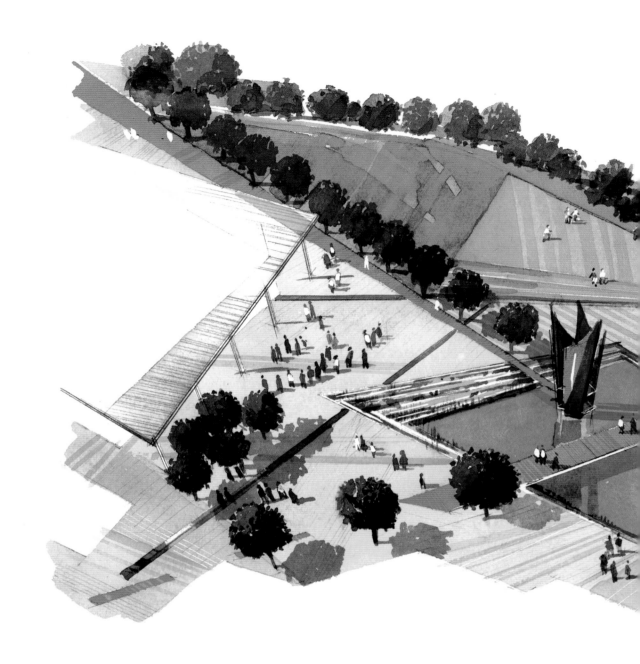

This design is an abstraction of the elements found in the Lincolnshire countryside. Sculpted earth is held by a limestone gabion wall whilst a bridge crosses the lake on axis with the view to the castle and cathedral.

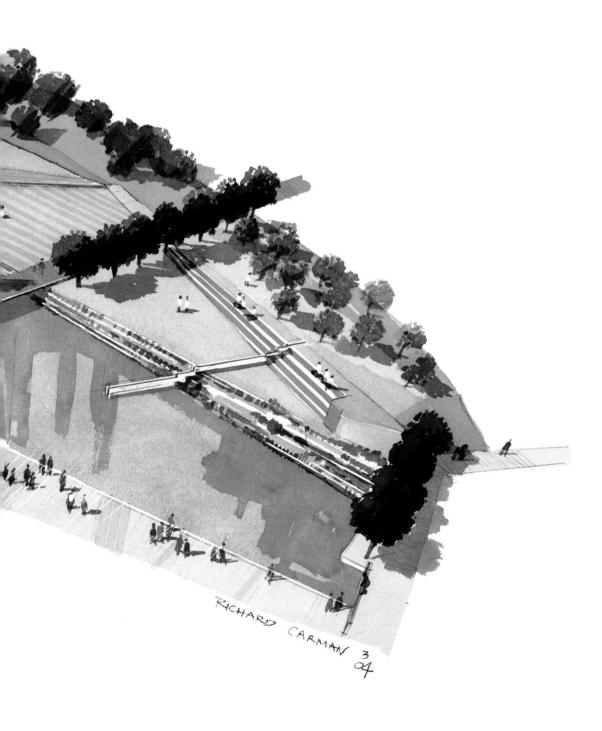

RICHARD CARMAN 3 04

Central Green Space and Delf Lake : Landscape Masterplan, University of Lincoln

The Arts Square

The design for the Arts Square draws reference from the Lincolnshire landscape. The abstract lines seen in the fenland fields have been re-interpreted by means of a dynamic composition of stone bands in the paving coupled with lines of trees. The layout creates a central space which obliquely addresses all the surrounding buildings. The iconic views to the castle and cathedral are captured, as the eye is guided along the main tree line towards Brayford Pool.

The square is cut by two linear hedges, each with trees planted within the hedge. One hedge line is cut through on the perpendicular by a mesh screen, which creates sub-spaces where seats have been located. The design encourages students to pause and socialise on their route through the campus. Stone block seats have been placed adjacent to the end wall of the East Midlands Media & Technology Enterprise Centre (EMMCTC) building, where it is envisaged that films will be shown outdoors.

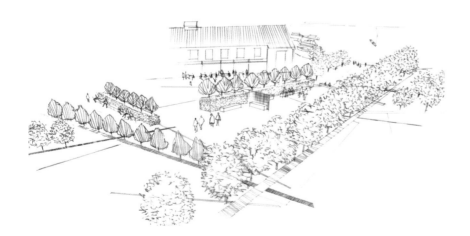

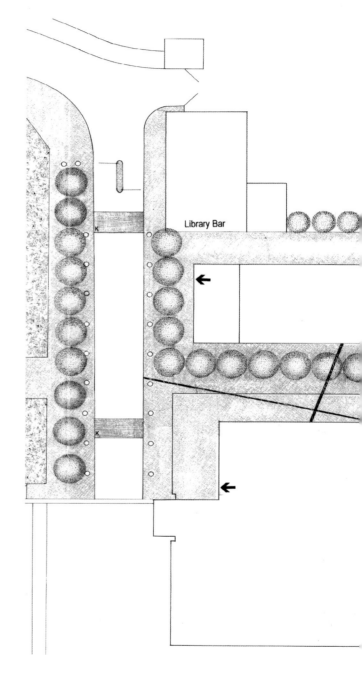

Library Bar

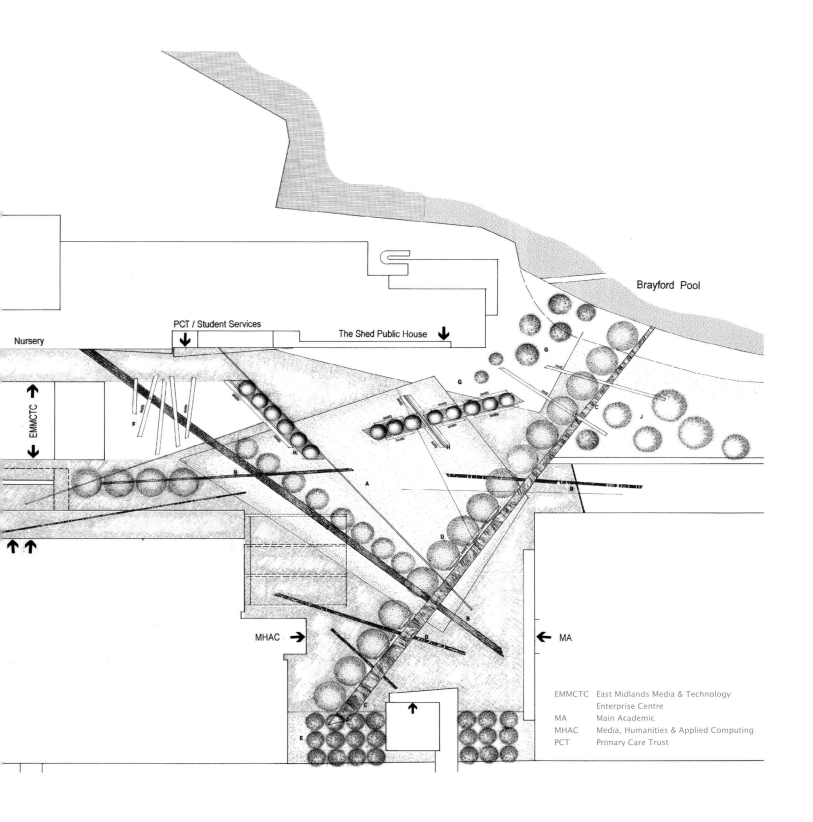

Brayford Pool

Nursery

PCT / Student Services

The Shed Public House

EMMCTC

F

H

A

G

G

C

J

B

B

D

D

B

MHAC

MA

C

E

EMMCTC   East Midlands Media & Technology
          Enterprise Centre
MA   Main Academic
MHAC   Media, Humanities & Applied Computing
PCT   Primary Care Trust

The Arts Square : Landscape Masterplan, University of Lincoln

St Clement's Park

Rochester Riverside

St Clement's Park, Rochester Riverside

'... the dark flat wilderness beyond the churchyard, intersected with dykes and mounds and gates, with scattered cattle feeding on it, was the marshes; and that the low leaden line beyond was the river; and that the distant savage lair from which the wind was rushing , was the sea ...'

Great Expectations by Charles Dickens

Rochester Riverside, is a series of neighbourhoods being developed across a 27-ha site which lies below the town, on former grazing marshland at the edge of the River Medway. Charles Dickens, a former resident of Rochester, sums up the sense of the wild in his book *Great Expectations*. Over time, boatyards and industries colonised the marshes, until 2000 when the industries were swept away and the land was raised above flood level and protected by a river wall. Although this has robbed the sense of the wild, the landscape design has captured the memory of the marsh to inspire the detail design.

St Clement's Park is part of a Landscape and Open Space Masterplan including a 2.5 km River Walk which leads to Crescent Park. The masterplan provides planning guidelines for the future implementation of the development.

The landscape context is striking, with Rochester Castle and Cathedral forming a dramatic backdrop. The site lies on a bend in the River with views downstream to the sculptural earthworks of Fort Amherst, Upnor Castle and Chatham Docks, which lie downstream on the banks of this fortified river. These remnants of militaria now appear sculptural and often surprising, with crisp earth embankments and walls of heroic scale. Vision corridors are retained, allowing the new park to be part of its unusual context. The design responds to this setting by using sculpted earth berms and changes in level to lead pedestrians through the park to the River Walk and focus views out over the Medway.

The marsh was covered with reeds and grasses, muddy creeks were held back by timber revetments, and the remains of old boats and rusting metal lay abandoned in the mud. This relic of the former marsh still had a story to tell; the site's rich history was tangible. These fragments of the past have been carefully collected to inspire the new landscape.

Top : image dated 1700, the marsh with the historic city on higher land to the rear
Bottom : map dated 1816 showing the site as grazing marshland

→ Views   **A** St Clement's Park   **B** River Walk   **C** Crescent Park

CREDITS
Client : Medway Council and SEEDA
Landscape Architects : Armstrong Bell Landscape Design
Landscape Managers : Land Management Services
Public Art Strategy : Artwise Curators
Date : 2006–08

Rochester Riverside lies on a bend in the River Medway with views downstream to Fort Amherst. The historic city of Rochester is visible on higher land to the rear.

Landscape Context : St Clement's Park, Rochester Riverside

The Design

The memory of the marsh is captured in the choice of materials which reference objects found abandoned in the mud

The design captures views to the river by creating three pedestrian routes which slide between buildings, connecting the park with the River Walk. The layout of the park, with its mobile dynamic of angled lines, is a direct response to these vision and movement lines. The memory of the marsh and the materials found there are reflected in the choice of materials used in the design. The main approach to St Clement's Park focuses on a Core-ten steel water wall, some 3 m in height and lit from the base at night. Core-ten steel references the rusting boats and remnants of former industry found on the site. A raised timber deck with a steel pergola and seating lies to the rear of the water wall, creating a layered effect when entering the park. The pergola is robust in appearance,

reminiscent of the former industries that occupied the site. On the ground plane, a composition of stone lines, lights set into the paving and low stone wall seats, reinforce the abstract geometry of the main movement lines. Sculpted earth embankments edge the park on two sides and are retained by sloping timber groynes, which make reference to the defensive earthworks at Fort Amherst. These embankments flank and frame the park, creating enclosure and privacy. They are planted with native grasses including *Deschampsia cespitosa*, inspired by the former grazing marshes. Birch trees are planted into the grasses whilst tight groups of Scots Pine are used at key locations to create visual accent and to lead the eye through to the river.

Development sketch showing the entrance to the park with Core-ten water wall and earth berms

Planted berms and a Core-ten water wall frame views into the park.
The steel pergola on a timber deck screens a play area to the rear.
A line of light set into the ground and stone wall seats form an
abstract geometry which leads the eye through to the river.

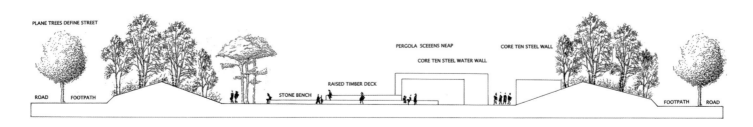

PLANE TREES DEFINE STREET

PERGOLA SCEEENS NEAP

CORE TEN STEEL WATER WALL

CORE TEN STEEL WALL

ROAD   FOOTPATH

STONE BENCH

RAISED TIMBER DECK

FOOTPATH   ROAD

The Park : perspective view and section
Section hand-drawn in ink on tracing paper

The Design : St Clement's Park, Rochester Riverside

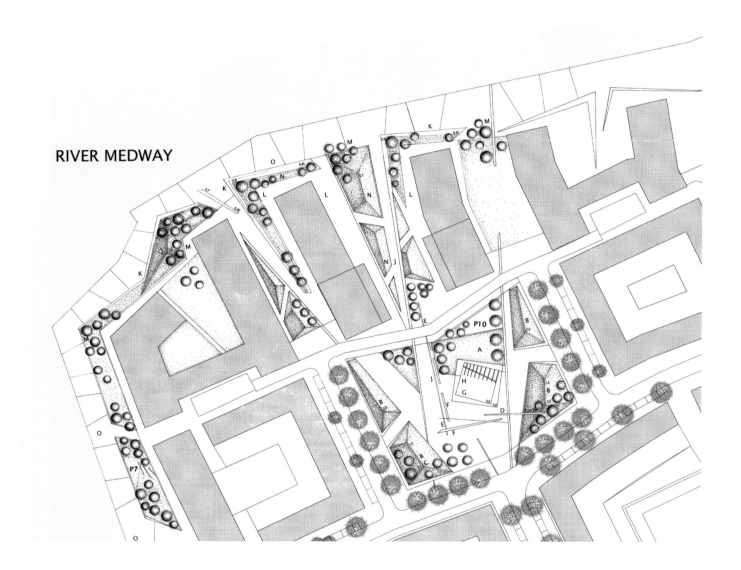

RIVER MEDWAY

A Children's play area
B Berms retained by timber groynes
C Birch trees and ornamental grasses
D Water wall in Core-ten steel
E In-ground lights direct view to river

F Low wall /seats
G Raised timber deck
H Steel pergola screens play area
J Sealed gravel cut by stone lines
K Stone wall/seats retain planting

L Timber decking semi-private
M Groups of birch and pine trees
N Ornamental grasses
O Sealed gravel cut by stone lines
Q Grass pyramid allows river views

Plan hand-drawn in ink on a CAD baseplan

The model   shows the abstract arrangement of
elements within the design when looking down at the
park from adjacent buildings

Plan and Model : St Clement's Park, Rochester Riverside

The 2.5 km River Walk connects St Clement's Park with Crescent Park further downstream. Sculpted earth berms planted with native grasses, are retained by stone wall seats which screen the River Walk from buildings to the rear. The soft landscape appears to push out between buildings, blurring the building line at the river's edge.

The River Walk, Rochester Riverside

Crescent Park
Rochester Riverside

Crescent Park, Rochester Riverside

An amphitheatre with a stage on the foreshore, designed for the Dickens Festival and other events

Crescent Park is part of the Landscape and Open Space Masterplan for Rochester Riverside and thererfore shares the same context described in St Clement's Park. The River Walk links St Clement's Park to Crescent Park further downstream. The park is set back in a semi–circular bay where the River Medway widens, with views downstream to the sculptural earthworks of Fort Amherst. The prevailing sense is that water dominates this landscape.

The Park is accessed from historic Rochester via Blue Boar Tunnel, which leads into a processional route to Crescent Park, connecting the old town with the new neighbourhood. Charles Dickens lived in Rochester for part of his life and set *Great Expectations* in the locality. The writer is still celebrated at the Dickens Festival, which holds annual processions and the new park is designed as a theatrical venue for this festival.

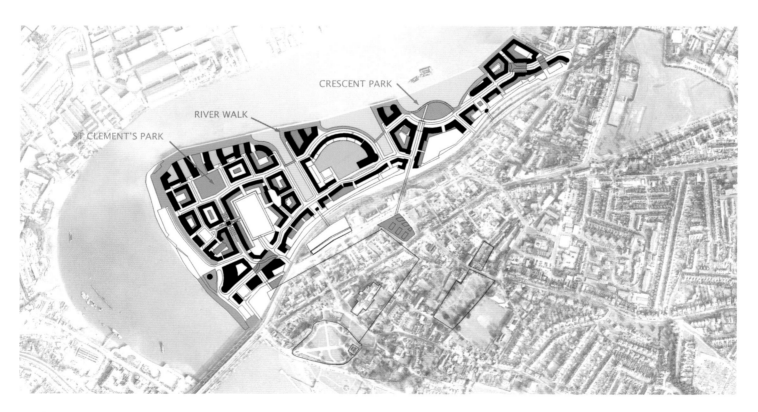

CRESCENT PARK

RIVER WALK

ST CLEMENT'S PARK

Rochester Riverside

CREDITS
Client : Medway Council and SEEDA
Landscape Architects : Armstrong Bell Landscape Design
Landscape Managers : Land Management Services
Public Art Consultants : Artwise Curators

The Dickens Festival in historic Rochester

The Dickens Festival : Crescent Park, Rochester Riverside

The Design

The land is sculpted and moulded, with lines of stone cutting through at angles, the stage almost hovering over the foreshore

Crescent Park has been designed as a performance space, for the Dickens Festival and other events. The land is sculpted into a semi-circular shallow bowl, which slopes gently down to the foreshore in a series of grass and stone steps. A timber boardwalk, designed as a stepped ramp, leads to a timber stage at the river's edge. The stage is set flush with the River Walk where the balustrade breaks, allowing access to the foreshore. When the tide is out, people can roam and get close to nature. Low walls provide seating and retain the grassed areas on either side of the bowl. The lines which form steps and low walls have been placed at angles to create an interplay and tension which makes the amphitheatre more lively and unexpected. The materials used in the design – stone, gravel, timber and Core-ten steel – are all derived from those found on the site, when it was former marshland. Pollarded willow trees are scattered on the upper slopes amongst a plantation of native grasses. The park is occasionally flooded with saline water and all specifications take account of this.

The River Medway, looking upstream towards Rochester

RICHARD CARMAN 12
06

The Design : Crescent Park, Rochester Riverside

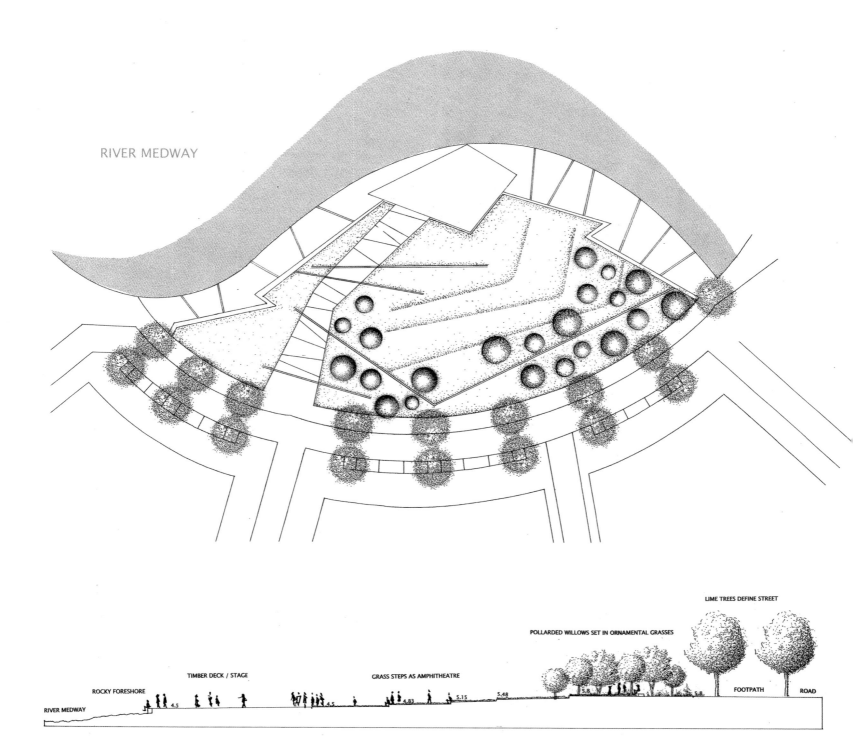

RIVER MEDWAY

LIME TREES DEFINE STREET

POLLARDED WILLOWS SET IN ORNAMENTAL GRASSES

TIMBER DECK / STAGE

GRASS STEPS AS AMPHITHEATRE

ROCKY FORESHORE

FOOTPATH

ROAD

RIVER MEDWAY

4.5   4.5   4.83   5.15   5.48   5.8   5.8

Plan and section hand-drawn in ink on tracing paper

The land is sculpted into steps with lines of
stone cutting through at angles. Trees frame
and hold the space at the upper level.

Plan, Section and Model : Crescent Park, Rochester Riverside

Clapham Gateway
London

Clapham Gateway, London

The historic heart of Old Town has been given back to pedestrians
and planted with eighty new trees

CREDITS
Client :
Lambeth Council and TFL
Architects : Marks Barfield Architects
Landscape Architects :
Armstrong Bell Landscape Design
Urban Design : Urban Initiatives
Traffic Engineer : The Project Centre
Main Contractor : FM Conway
Date : 2013

Plans and visualisations all by kind
permission of Marks Barfield Architects

AWARDS
Civic Trust Awards 2016 :
Regional Finalist
New London Architecture Awards
2015 :Public Space
London Planning Award 2015 :
Best Public Space
Placemaking Awards 2015 :
Highly Commended for Design

Clapham Old Town is a conservation area at the historic heart of Clapham, framed by Georgian and Victorian buildings with the small scale Polygon buildings at the centre. The southern end of the space connects to Clapham Common, with views to historic Holy Trinity Church. The space had evolved in an ad hoc way and the increase in traffic and use of the space as a bus stand, had created conflicts of interest.

The project creates a new piazza, where the dominance of traffic has been significantly reduced by removing the gyratory system and re-designing the bus stand layout, which gives the area back to pedestrians. The scheme was taken to public consultation and gained the backing of local people.

The piazza is edged with a line of new plane trees, which visually connect with an existing line of mature plane trees edging the Common, bringing a feeling of the Common into the space. A planter at the north end of the space partially screens the bus stand and is planted with native *Deschampsia cespitosa* grasses, threaded through with herbaceous plants and multi-stem *Amelanchier* trees. *Catalpa nana* trees shelter a scattering of individual chairs across the Yorkstone and free-draining gravel paving. These small-scale trees reflect the domestic character of the Polygon buildings and create an informal feeling. Eighty new trees have been planted in the piazza and adjacent streets, which have had the effect of softening and greening Clapham Old Town.

The scheme as depicted in the following images shows our design intent. The installation of the scheme was carried out and supervised by Lambeth Council as a design and build contract, and differs in detail.

All the plans and computer generated visualisations shown here, were prepared by Marks Barfield Architects.

THE SITE

Aerial view of the site before the scheme was carried out. Clapham Common
and Holy Trinity Church are visible at the bottom of the image.

Introduction : Clapham Gateway, London

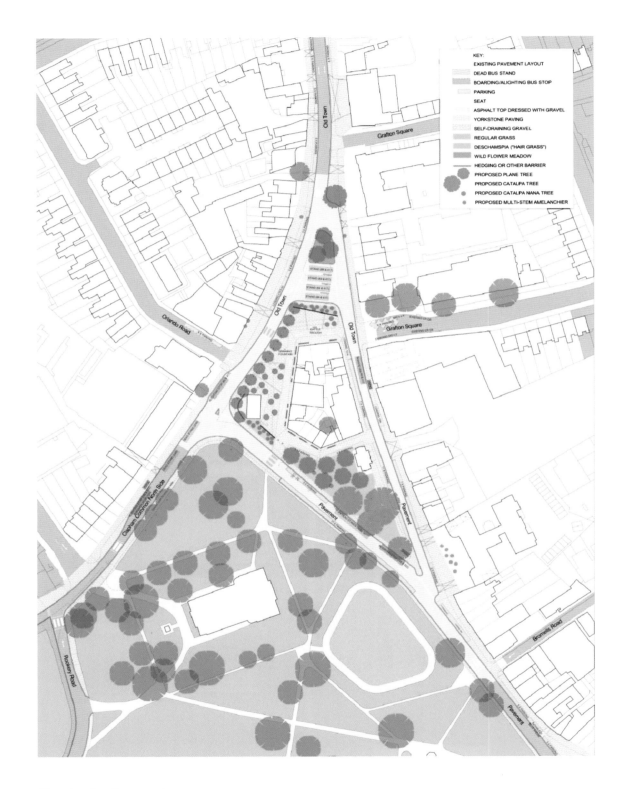

KEY:
EXISTING PAVEMENT LAYOUT
DEAD BUS STAND
BOARDING/ALIGHTING BUS STOP
PARKING
SEAT
ASPHALT TOP DRESSED WITH GRAVEL
YORKSTONE PAVING
SELF-DRAINING GRAVEL
REGULAR GRASS
DESCHAMSPIA ("HAIR GRASS")
WILD FLOWER MEADOW
HEDGING OR OTHER BARRIER
PROPOSED PLANE TREE
PROPOSED CATALPA TREE
PROPOSED CATALPA NANA TREE
PROPOSED MULTI-STEM AMELANCHIER

Plan showing the new piazza

After : the new piazza with tree planting

Before : the space is dominated by roads and car parking

Before and After : Clapham Gateway, London

The piazza is screened from the bus stand by a plantation of native grasses with multi-stem *Amelanchier* trees. Plane trees seen on the left edge of the piazza, add structure whilst making a visual connection with Clapham Common. The space is paved with high quality Yorkstone and free-draining gravel.

Visualisation of the Piazza : Clapham Gateway, London

View looking north with the Polygon buildings on
the right and *Catalpa nana* trees in the foreground

View looking south towards Clapham Common
with Holy Trinity Church in the background

Visualisation of the Piazza : Clapham Gateway, London

Left : Planting shelters the piazza from the road
Right : The Trinity Restaurant looks towards the Common

Left : Street tree planting greens Old Town
Right : Mature plane trees edge the Common,
new plane trees continue into the piazza

Images this page and opposite : Diana Armstrong Bell

The Piazza : Clapham Gateway, London

Further Reading

These books and exhibition catalogues are just a small and diverse selection of the many books in my own library that I turn to regularly for inspiration or information

Art

Anselm Kiefer, Royal Academy, 2014 catalogue

Borchardt-Hume, Achim, *Malevich,* Tate Publishing, 2014 catalogue

Chambers, Emma and Karin Orchard, *Schwitters in Britain,* Tate Publishing (2013)

Cork, Richard, *Ann Christopher,* Royal Academy (2016)

El Lissitzky, *A Suprematist Tale of Two Squares in Six Constructions,* Tate Publishing (2014), reprinted in English

Fischer, Hartwig and Sean Rainbird, *Kandinsky – The Path to Abstraction,* Tate Publishing, 2006 catalogue

Lewison, Jeremy, *Ben Nicholson,* Tate Gallery, 1993 catalogue

Martin, J.L., Ben Nicholson and N. Gabo, *Circle – International Survey of Constructive Art,* Praeger Publishers (1971)

Milner, John, *Kazimir Malevich and the Art of Geometry,* Yale University Press (1996)

Milner, John, *El Lissitzky Design,* Antique Collectors Club (2009)

Passuth, Krisztina, *Moholy-Nagy,* Thames and Hudson (1985)

Architecture

Curtis, William J. R., *Alvaro Siza 1995–1999,* El Croquis (1999)

Droste, Magdalena, *The Bauhaus 1919–1933,* Taschen (2019)

Hadid, Zaha, *Zaha Hadid – The Complete Buildings and Projects,* Thames and Hudson (1998)

Zaha Hadid, Guggenheim Museum, 2006 catalogue

Zaha Hadid – *Early Paintings and Drawings,* Serpentine Galleries, Koenig Books (2016)

Kipnis, Jeffrey and Anthony Vidler, *Daniel Libeskind – the Space of Encounter,* Thames and Hudson (2001)

Miralles Tagliabue, Editorial Gustavo Gili, Sa, Barcelona (1999), magazine monograph, Time Architecture

Zanco, Federica, *Luis Barragan – the Quiet Revolution,* Skira editore (2001) Barragan Foundation

Landscape

Arnold, Henry F., *Trees in Urban Design*, Van Nostrand Reinhold Company (1980)

Balmori, Diana, *A Landscape Manifesto*, Yale University Press (2010)

Bradley-Hole, Christopher, *The Minimalist Garden*, Mitchell Beazley (1999)

Dempsey, Amy, *Destination Art*, Thames and Hudson (2006 and 2011)

Farjon, Aljos, *Ancient Oaks in the English Landscape*, Royal Botanic Gardens (Kew 2017)

Masson, Georgina, *Italian Gardens*, Antique Collectors Club (1987)

Rackham, Oliver, *The Illustrated History of the Countryside*, Weidenfeld and Nicholson (2003)

Spens, Michael, *Gardens of the Mind – the Genius of Geoffrey Jellicoe*, Antique Collectors Club (1992)

Nature / Landscape Writing

Baker, J A, *The Peregrine – The Hill of Summer and Diaries*, Harper Collins Publishers (2011)

Deakin, Roger, *Wildwood, a Journey through trees*, Penguin Books (2007)

Macfarlane, Robert, *The Old Ways – a journey on foot*, Hamish Hamilton (2012)
… and all his other books.

Further Reading